THE
HUMAN
SEASON

SELECTED POEMS 1926–1972

Also by Archibald MacLeish

Poems

Collected Poems, 1917–1952
Songs for Eve
"The Wild Old Wicked Man" & Other Poems

Plays in Verse

Panic
The Fall of the City
Air Raid
The Trojan Horse
This Music Crept by Me upon the Waters
J.B.
Herakles

Play in Prose

Scratch

Prose

The Irresponsibles
The American Cause
A Time to Speak
A Time to Act
American Opinion and the War
Poetry and Opinion
Freedom Is the Right to Choose
Poetry and Experience
The Eleanor Roosevelt Story
A Continuing Journey

THE
HUMAN
SEASON

SELECTED POEMS 1926–1972

ARCHIBALD
MacLEISH

HOUGHTON MIFFLIN
COMPANY · BOSTON

Third Printing w

Copyright © 1972 by Archibald MacLeish

Library of Congress Catalog Card Number: 72–1107
ISBN: 0–395–13943–0

Printed in the United States of America

FOREWORD

A T EIGHTY you have to begin to look ahead. What will be left when they carry you off? Your work, you tell yourself. But will your work be left? I have written some twenty volumes of verse over the past fifty years but I know better than to suppose they will still be around on the shelves when I'm out of print myself. Poems these days are read in anthologies — even taught from anthologies — which means that what will remain is the anthological grist, the eight or ten poems (usually the same eight or ten) chosen for one anthology or another in a life's time.

I am not complaining. The same thing has happened to better men than I. There must be millions of former students of English to whom Yeats himself is the poet of a handful of anthology pieces including — God save us! — the poem he detested, "The Lake Isle of Innisfree." But even without complaining one can permit one's self to observe that it's a curious way to approach an art. You wouldn't attempt to get at Dean Swift by sample pages — even your favorite sample pages. Why then should you try it in poetry? A book of poems is not a bouquet from which to pick a choice of posies. A book of poems is an attempt to come to terms with the experiences of a mortal life and it is almost always a whole thing — as whole in its way as a well-made novel. Take any of Stevens' volumes, any of Frost's, Eliot's: the work is not in the familiar choices but in the entire book.

And it is there that the anthology, however valuable for other purposes, fails. A student reader — and there are more student readers of poetry in our society than we suspect — may catch a hint of the tune in one poem or another, but because there is usually nothing around but the class anthology he will have nowhere to turn for a further go — an extension of the conversation. And the result is failure in all directions: failure for the student reader's interest, failure for the teacher's purpose, failure for the poet's hope. For a poet like a novelist or a critic or anyone else hopes to be read, not tasted.

It is for that reason, I suppose, that selections of poems like this one have become more frequent. A fair selection should give a generation raised on samples a means of getting through to the work itself without consulting catalogue cards or collected texts. And, at the same time, it should give the exhibits in the anthologies a chance to speak for themselves. For the process of selection is of course the opposite of the process of anthologizing: not a choice *from* but a representation *of*. In this book, for example, there are a number of more or less autobiographical poems which have never appeared in anthologies

vi

but which are included here because they represent attempts to come to terms with the tragic sense of time and change which afflicted the generation of the two Great Wars, the wars of the fall of the old world. And here too, and for the same reason, are poems on that curious theme which began to trouble Americans in my generation as a consequence of their confrontation with Europe in their service in France during the First War and their life in Paris afterward: the "strangeness" of being "American." Anthologies might well ignore both — indeed they generally do — but a fair representation of the work of any member of my American generation would have to deal with each of them and with the new face of love in that time and the new — at least different — face of art.

With a selection on this basis the poems propose themselves, and not because they are "better" but because they are more themselves — more "like it." When the work started, when the polls opened, I thought often of Frost's title for his selection, *Aforesaid*, and, as always, I envied him. Now that the selection is made I see that, even if I had had the wit to think of it, *Aforesaid* would not have been right. What this book says I never said before. It's not my story, it's the poems': what they think they know when they put themselves together.

Archibald MacLeish

Conway, Massachusetts

CONTENTS

ACTORS AND SCENES

LOVE AND NOT

"STRANGE THING . . . TO BE AN AMERICAN"

ILLUSTRATIONS

THE ART

NEWS FROM ELSEWHERE

AUTO-
BIOGRAPHY
AND
OMENS

YACHT FOR SALE

My youth is
Made fast
To the dock
At Marseilles
Rotting away
With a chain to her mast,

She that saw slaughters
In foreign waters:

She that was torn
With the winds off the Horn:

She that was beached in the bleaching environs
Of sirens:

She that rounded the Cape of Good Hope
With a rope's aid:

She's fast there
Off the Cannebière.

It's easy to see
She was frail in the knee
And too sharp in the bow —
You can see now.

LINES FOR A PROLOGUE

These alternate nights and days, these seasons
Somehow fail to convince me. It seems
I have the sense of infinity!

(In your dreams, O crew of Columbus,
O listeners over the sea
For the surf that breaks upon Nothing —)

Once I was waked by the nightingales in the garden.
I thought, What time is it? I thought,
Time — Is it Time still? — Now is it Time?

(Tell me your dreams, O sailors:
Tell me, in sleep did you climb
The tall masts, and before you —)

At night the stillness of old trees
Is a leaning over and the inertness
Of hills is a kind of waiting.

(In sleep, in a dream, did you see
The world's end? Did the water
Break — and no shore — Did you see?)

Strange faces come through the streets to me
Like messengers: and I have been warned
By the moving slowly of hands at a window.

Oh, I have the sense of infinity —
But the world, sailors, is round.
They say there is no end to it.

L'AN TRENTIESME DE MON EAGE

And I have come upon this place
By lost ways, by a nod, by words,
By faces, by an old man's face
At Morlaix lifted to the birds,

By hands upon the tablecloth
At Aldebori's, by the thin
Child's hands that opened to the moth
And let the flutter of the moonlight in,

By hands, by voices, by the voice
Of Mrs. Whitman on the stair,
By Margaret's "If we had the choice
To choose or not —" through her thick hair,

By voices, by the creak and fall
Of footsteps on the upper floor,
By silence waiting in the hall
Between the doorbell and the door,

By words, by voices, a lost way —
And here above the chimney stack
The unknown constellations sway —
And by what way shall I go back?

LE SECRET HUMAIN

It was not God that told us. We knew
Before, long before, long, long ago.
We knew that tonight — or tomorrow . . . We know
Still — tomorrow. It is true that we know.

The incredulous surprise
In the faces of the dead, in dead eyes:
There was something still to happen —
There was someone that was always going to come.

And the eyes of those that sleep,
The puzzled eyes:
There are promises the silence does not keep —
And the dark has no replies.

Ah, we know
As the wind blows,
Not to the south, the north,
Not to, not ever to, but toward.

We know beyond the doors we press and open,
Beyond the smell of breakfast in the hall,
Beyond the soggy towel and the soap —
Wait! We shall know all.

We that sit and think and talk,
We that lie awake till late,
We that walk beside the river:
We can wait — Oh we can wait!

AUTOBIOGRAPHY

from *The Hamlet of A. MacLeish*

We have learned the answers, all the answers:
It is the question that we do not know.

Night after night I lie like this listening.
Night after night I cannot sleep. I wake
Knowing something, thinking something has happened.
I have this feeling a great deal. I have
Sadness often. At night I have this feeling.
Waking I feel this pain as though I knew
Something not to be thought of, something unbearable.
I feel this pain at night as though some
Terrible thing had happened. At night the sky
Opens, the near things vanish, the bright walls
Fall, and the stars were always there, and the dark
There and the cold and the stillness. I wake and stand
A long time by the window. I always think
The trees know the way they are silent. I always
Think some one has spoken, some one has told me.
Reading the books I always think so, reading
Words overheard in the books, reading the words
Like words in a strange language. I always hear
Music like that. I almost remember with music . . .
This is not what you think. It is not that. I swim
Every day at the beach under the fig tree.
I swim very well and far out. The smell
Of pine comes over the water. The wind blurs
Seaward. And afternoons I walk to the phare.
Much of the time I do not think anything;
Much of the time I do not even notice.

And then, speaking, closing a door, I see
Strangely as though I almost saw now, some
Shape of things I have always seen, the sun
White on a house and the windows open and swallows
In and out of the wallpaper, the moon's face
Faint by day in a mirror; I see some
Changed thing that is telling, something that almost
Tells — and this pain then, then this pain. And no
Words, only these shapes of things that seem
Ways of knowing what it is I am knowing.
I write these things in books, on pieces of paper.
I have written "The wind rises . . ." I have written "Bells
Plunged in the wind . . ." I have written "Like
Doors . . ." "Like evening . . ."
It is always the same: I cannot read what the words say.
It is always the same: there are signs and I cannot read
        them.
There are empty streets and the blinds drawn and the sky
Sliding in windows. There are lights before
Dawn in the yellow transoms over the doors.
There are steps that pass and pass all night that are
        always
One, always the same step passing . . .
I have traveled a great deal. I have seen at Homs
The cranes over the river and Isfahan
The fallen tiles in the empty garden, and Shiraz
Far off, the cypresses under the hill.
It is always the same. I have seen on the Kazvin road
On the moon grey desert the leafless wind,
The wind raging in moon-dusk. Or the light that comes
Seaward with slow oars from the mouth of Euphrates.
I have heard the nightingales in the thickets of Gilan,
And at dawn, at Teheran, I have heard from the ancient

Westward greying face of the wandering planet
The voices calling the small new name of god,
The voices answered with cockcrow, answered at dusk
With the cry of jackals far away in the gardens.
I have heard the name of the moon beyond those
      mountains.
It is always the same. It is always as though some
Smell of leaves had made me not quite remember;
As though I had turned to look and there were no one.
It has always been secret like that with me.
Always something has not been said. Always
The stones were there, the trees were there, the
      motionless
Hills have appeared in the dusk to me, the moon
Has stood a long time white and still in the window.
Always the earth has been turned away from me hiding
The veiled eyes and the wind in the leaves has not
      spoken . . .

As now the night is still. As the night now
Stands at the farthest off of touch and like
A raised hand held upon the empty air
Means and is silent.
               Look! It waves me still . . .
    I say Go on! Go on!
                    As the whole night now
Made visible behind this darkness seems
To beckon to me . . .

WAGONS-LITS

The incoherent rushing of the train
Dulls like a drugged pain

Numbs
To an ether throbbing of inaudible drums

Unfolds
Hush within hush until the night withholds

Only its darkness.
                    From the deep
Dark a voice calls like a voice in sleep

Slowly a strange name in a strange tongue.

Among

The sleeping listeners a sound
As leaves stir faintly on the ground

When snow falls from a windless sky —
A stir   A sigh

"LE SEUL MALHEUR EST QUE
JE NE SAIS PAS LIRE"

In the doorway of the Bar
Du Bon Port at Saint Tropez
Sharp against the light
The old sailor in the fez

Stands face upward to the stars.
Is it I then, only I,
I who have such need to know,
I alone that cannot read?

ELEVEN

And summer mornings the mute child, rebellious,
Stupid, hating the words, the meanings, hating
The Think now, Think, the Oh but Think! would leave
On tiptoe the three chairs on the verandah
And crossing tree by tree the empty lawn
Push back the shed door and upon the sill
Stand pressing out the sunlight from his eyes
And enter and with outstretched fingers feel
The grindstone and behind it the bare wall
And turn and in the corner on the cool
Hard earth sit listening. And one by one,

12

Out of the dazzled shadow in the room,
The shapes would gather, the brown plowshare, spades,
Mattocks, the polished helves of picks, a scythe
Hung from the rafters, shovels, slender tines
Glinting across the curve of sickles — shapes
Older than men were, the wise tools, the iron
Friendly with earth. And sit there, quiet, breathing
The harsh dry smell of withered bulbs, the faint
Odor of dung, the silence. And outside
Beyond the half-shut door the blind leaves
And the corn moving. And at noon would come,
Up from the garden, his hard crooked hands
Gentle with earth, his knees still earth-stained, smelling
Of sun, of summer, the old gardener, like
A priest, like an interpreter, and bend
Over his baskets.
   And they would not speak:
They would say nothing. And the child would sit there
Happy as though he had no name, as though
He had been no one: like a leaf, a stem,
Like a root growing —

MISTRAL OVER THE GRAVES

Be still — listen to the wind!
Listen to the night wind slithering and splashing
In the palm trees, in the poplars —
Saying Ah, Ah, in the pine trees —
Listen to the wind! Be still!

Be still — listen to the wind.
There is no sound at all but the wind now,
No sleepless sound of old men coughing,
No knocking of little iron nails upon the stones.
Listen to the wind! Be still!

Be still — listen to the wind.
The sound of live men on the earth is the rustling
Of small mice in a windy barn.

Listen to the wind, Dead Heart, at the closed door —
Listen to the wind! Be still!

THE SILENT SLAIN

for Kenneth MacLeish, 1894–1918

We too, we too, descending once again
The hills of our own land, we too have heard
Far off — Ah, que ce cor a longue haleine —
The horn of Roland in the passages of Spain,
The first, the second blast, the failing third,
And with the third turned back and climbed once more
The steep road southward, and heard faint the sound
Of swords, of horses, the disastrous war,
And crossed the dark defile at last, and found
At Roncevaux upon the darkening plain
The dead against the dead and on the silent ground
The silent slain —

MEMORIAL RAIN

for Kenneth MacLeish

Ambassador Puser the ambassador
Reminds himself in French, felicitous tongue,
What these (young men no longer) lie here for
In rows that once, and somewhere else, were young . . .

All night in Brussels the wind had tugged at my door:
I had heard the wind at my door and the trees strung
Taut, and to me who had never been before
In that country it was a strange wind, blowing
Steadily, stiffening the walls, the floor,
The roof of my room. I had not slept for knowing
He too, dead, was a stranger in that land
And felt beneath the earth in the wind's flowing
A tightening of roots and would not understand,
Remembering lake winds in Illinois,
That strange wind. I had felt his bones in the sand
Listening.

     . . . Reflects that these enjoy
Their country's gratitude, that deep repose,
That peace no pain can break, no hurt destroy,
That rest, that sleep . . .

                At Ghent the wind rose.
There was a smell of rain and a heavy drag
Of wind in the hedges but not as the wind blows
Over fresh water when the waves lag
Foaming and the willows huddle and it will rain:
I felt him waiting.

. . . Indicates the flag
Which (may he say) enisles in Flanders plain
This little field these happy, happy dead
Have made America . . .

                      In the ripe grain
The wind coiled glistening, darted, fled,
Dragging its heavy body: at Waereghem
The wind coiled in the grass above his head:
Waiting — listening . . .

        . . . Dedicates to them
This earth their bones have hallowed, this last gift
A grateful country . . .

                Under the dry grass stem
The words are blurred, are thickened, the words sift
Confused by the rasp of the wind, by the thin grating
Of ants under the grass, the minute shift
And tumble of dusty sand separating
From dusty sand. The roots of the grass strain,
Tighten, the earth is rigid, waits — he is waiting —

And suddenly, and all at once, the rain!

THE YOUNG DEAD SOLDIERS

for Lieutenant Richard Myers

The young dead soldiers do not speak.
Nevertheless, they are heard in the still houses: who has
    not heard them?
They have a silence that speaks for them at night and
    when the clock counts.
They say: We were young. We have died. Remember
    us.
They say: We have done what we could but until it is
    finished it is not done.
They say: We have given our lives but until it is finished
    no one can know what our lives gave.
They say: Our deaths are not ours; they are yours; they
    will mean what you make them.
They say: Whether our lives and our deaths were for
    peace and a new hope or for nothing we cannot
    say; it is you who must say this.
They say: We leave you our deaths. Give them their
    meaning.
We were young, they say. We have died. Remember us.

SIGNATURE FOR TEMPO

Think that this world against the wind of time
Perpetually falls the way a hawk
Falls at the wind's edge but is motionless —

Think that this silver snail the moon will climb
All night upon time's curving stalk
That as she climbs bends, bends beneath her —

                                                Yes

And think that we remember the past time.

VERSES FOR A CENTENNIAL

The birthplace of Mr. William Shakespeare author
Of Timon and other poetry including
"Who sees his true love on her naked bed
Teaching the sheets" including also sonnets
"To one of one still such and ever so"
Or Lincoln's in Kentucky where they say,
From This to That: Think of it! (If they could!)
Or Dante Alighieri's — Godi Fiorenza —
Has not been found. They cannot fix their marbles
Just where the year twelve hundred sixty five
Rolled up the Arno or where time and Troy
And Stratford crossed each other. On this spot —
    Where now, where now along the great ecliptic
    Traced by a wandering planet that unwinds
    Space into hours? —
                  Upon this very spot

The year of Christ one thousand five six four —
And of Erasmus four score seventeen —
And Leonardo one one two —

                                   was born —
To P. Ovidius Naso and the queen
Lying in Florida on a Venetian bed
Carved with the loves of Venus —
William Shakespeare.

THE END OF THE WORLD

Quite unexpectedly as Vasserot
The armless ambidextrian was lighting
A match between his great and second toe
And Ralph the lion was engaged in biting
The neck of Madame Sossman while the drum
Pointed, and Teeny was about to cough
In waltz-time swinging Jocko by the thumb —
Quite unexpectedly the top blew off:

And there, there overhead, there, there, hung over
Those thousands of white faces, those dazed eyes,
There in the starless dark the poise, the hover,
There with vast wings across the canceled skies,
There in the sudden blackness the black pall
Of nothing, nothing, nothing — nothing at all.

EPISTLE TO BE LEFT IN THE EARTH

... It is colder now,
                    there are many stars,
                                    we are drifting
North by the Great Bear,
                        the leaves are falling,
The water is stone in the scooped rocks,
                              to southward
Red sun grey air:
                  the crows are
Slow on their crooked wings,
                        the jays have left us:
Long since we passed the flares of Orion.
Each man believes in his heart he will die.
Many have written last thoughts and last letters.
None know if our deaths are now or forever:
None know if this wandering earth will be found.
We lie down and the snow covers our garments.

I pray you,
                you (if any open this writing)
Make in your mouths the words that were our names.

I will tell you all we have learned,
                              I will tell you everything:
The earth is round,
                      there are springs under the orchards,
The loam cuts with a blunt knife,
                        beware of
Elms in thunder,
                the lights in the sky are stars —

We think they do not see,
                    we think also
The trees do not know nor the leaves of the grasses
        hear us:
The birds too are ignorant.
                        Do not listen.
Do not stand at dark in the open windows.
We before you have heard this:
                        they are voices:
They are not words at all but the wind rising.
Also none among us has seen God.
(. . . We have thought often
The flaws of sun in the late and driving weather
Pointed to one tree but it was not so.)
As for the nights I warn you the nights are dangerous:
The wind changes at night and the dreams come.

It is very cold,
                there are strange stars near Arcturus,

Voices are crying an unknown name in the sky

MEN

(on a phrase of Apollinaire)

Our history is grave noble and tragic.
We trusted the look of the sun on the green leaves.
We built our towns of stone with enduring ornaments.
We worked the hard flint for basins of water.

We believed in the feel of the earth under us.
We planted corn grapes apple trees rhubarb.
Nevertheless we knew others had died.
Everything we have done has been faithful and dangerous.

We believed in the promises made by the brows of
    women.
We begot children at night in the warm wool.
We comforted those who wept in fear on our shoulders.
Those who comforted us had themselves vanished.

We fought at the dikes in the bright sun for the pride
    of it.
We beat drums and marched with music and laughter.
We were drunk and lay with our fine dreams in the
    straw.
We saw the stars through the hair of lewd women.

Our history is grave noble and tragic.
Many of us have died and are not remembered.
Many cities are gone and their channels broken.
We have lived a long time in this land and with honor.

IMMORTAL AUTUMN

I speak this poem now with grave and level voice
In praise of autumn, of the far-horn-winding fall.

I praise the flower-barren fields, the clouds, the tall
Unanswering branches where the wind makes sullen noise.

I praise the fall: it is the human season.
                                        Now
No more the foreign sun does meddle at our earth,
Enforce the green and bring the fallow land to birth,
Nor winter yet weigh all with silence the pine bough,

But now in autumn with the black and outcast crows
Share we the spacious world: the whispering year is gone:
There is more room to live now: the once secret dawn
Comes late by daylight and the dark unguarded goes.

Between the mutinous brave burning of the leaves
And winter's covering of our hearts with his deep snow
We are alone: there are no evening birds: we know
The naked moon: the tame stars circle at our eaves.

It is the human season. On this sterile air
Do words outcarry breath: the sound goes on and on.
I hear a dead man's cry from autumn long since gone.

I cry to you beyond upon this bitter air.

YOU, ANDREW MARVELL

And here face down beneath the sun
And here upon earth's noonward height
To feel the always coming on
The always rising of the night:

To feel creep up the curving east
The earthy chill of dusk and slow
Upon those under lands the vast
And ever climbing shadow grow

And strange at Ecbatan the trees
Take leaf by leaf the evening strange
The flooding dark about their knees
The mountains over Persia change

And now at Kermanshah the gate
Dark empty and the withered grass
And through the twilight now the late
Few travelers in the westward pass

And Baghdad darken and the bridge
Across the silent river gone
And through Arabia the edge
Of evening widen and steal on

And deepen on Palmyra's street
The wheel rut in the ruined stone
And Lebanon fade out and Crete
High through the clouds and overblown

And over Sicily the air
Still flashing with the landward gulls

And loom and slowly disappear
The sails above the shadowy hulls

And Spain go under and the shore
Of Africa the gilded sand
And evening vanish and no more
The low pale light across that land

Nor now the long light on the sea:

And here face downward in the sun
To feel how swift how secretly
The shadow of the night comes on . . .

SHIP'S LOG

What islands known, what passages discovered,
Rocks seen from far off to leeward,
Low, a few palms, odor of sandalwood,
The whole thing blue with dusk . . .

Mostly I have relinquished and forgotten
Or grown accustomed, which is a way of forgetting.
The more I have travelled the less I have departed.
I had foreseen the unicorn, the nose-rings.

Once in my youth I bailed ship and launched her
As a blue-jay bolts from an apple-tree.
Now I go but have not gone:
Troy is Ithaca again but farther.

26

Only the young, on a first voyage, facing the
Whole horizon of the sea
Depart from any country. The old men
Sail to the sea-beach they have left behind.

LA FOCE

Close the shutters. Let the ceiling fly
dance around the chandelier
in silent circles with inaudible small cry
in celebration of my seventieth year.

Why grow older in a Tuscan spring
where everything,
follies and flowers, loves and leaves,
grows younger and the loam conceives
and even the slow venerable sun
splashes in the water spills
and hills
invent again the new
first blue?

Close the shutters. Tuscan noon.
A hen upon the barley ground
tells the welkin what her industry has found

and heaven answers. All must run,
Yeats tells us, backward to be new begun
as does the silver bullion of the moon.

Only one small circling fly
remembers that the world goes by
and we go with it
                          he and I.

THE OLD MEN
IN THE LEAF SMOKE

The old men rake the yards for winter
Burning the autumn-fallen leaves.
They have no lives, the one or the other.
The leaves are dead, the old men live
Only a little, light as a leaf,
Left to themselves of all their loves:
Light in the head most often too.

Raking the leaves, raking the lives,
Raking life and leaf together,
The old men smell of burning leaves,
But which is which they wonder — whether
Anyone tells the leaves and loves —
Anyone left, that is, who lives.

THEY COME NO MORE, THOSE
WORDS, THOSE FINCHES

Oh when you're young
And the words to your tongue
Like the birds to Saint Francis
With darting, with dances —
Wait! you say, Wait!
There's still time! It's not late!

And the next day you're old
And the words all as cold
As the birds in October
Sing over, sing over,
Sing Late! Late!

And Wait! you say, Wait!

WHAT THE OLD
WOMEN SAY

Out there in the fighting
Each day is doubt,
Each night is dread,
Dawn is disaster.

Even at home in the house
If the lock creeps in the socket
The roots of our sleep wake.
We lie listening.

Like flood in a field it comes —
No sound but suddenly
One more stone has vanished,
A dyke drowned.

Never again in our lifetime,
Never will fear end
Or the old ease return to us:
Childhood remembered.

Never again will we wait
Content in the dark till our daughters
Off in the evening somewhere,
Laughing, come home.

COMPANIONS

The flowers with the ragged names,
daffodils and such,
met us on the road we came,
nodded, touched.

Now, the golden day gone by,
we walk the other road:
they throng the evening grass beside,
touch us . . .
                    nod.

SURVIVOR

On an oak in autumn
there'll always be
one leaf left at the top of the tree
that won't let go with the rest and rot —
won't cast loose and skitter and sail
and end in a puddle of rain in a swale
and fatten the earth and be fruitful . . .
                                    No,
it won't and it won't and it won't let go.
It rattles a kind of a jig tattoo,
a telegrapher's tattle that *will* get through
like an SOS from a struggling ship
over and over, a dash and a skip.

You cover your head with your quilt and still
that telegrapher's key on Conway hill
calls to Polaris.

I can spell:
I know what it says . . . I know too well.
I pull my pillow over my ear
but I hear.

ACTORS
AND SCENES

BERNÁL DÍAZ

from Bernál Díaz' Preface to His Book *Conquistador*

"That which I have myself seen and the fighting" . . .

And I am an ignorant man: and this priest this
Gómara with the school-taught skip to his writing

The pompous Latin the appropriate feasts
The big names the imperial decorations
The beautiful battles and the brave deceased

35

The onward marches the wild Indian nations
The conquests sieges sorties wars campaigns
(And one eye always on the live relations) —

He with his famous history of New Spain —
This priest is a learned man: is not ignorant:
And I am poor: without gold: gainless:

My lands deserts in Guatemala: my fig-tree the
Spiked bush: my grapes thorns: my children
Half-grown: sons with beards: the big one

Breaking the small of his back in the brothel thills
And a girl to be married and all of them snarling at
          home
With the Indian look in their eyes like a cat killing:

And this Professor Francisco López de Gómara
Childless; not poor: and I am old: over eighty:
Stupid with sleepless nights: unused to the combing of

Words clean of the wool while the tale waits:
And he is a youthful man: a sound one: lightened with
Good sleep: skilled in the pen's plaiting —

I am an ignorant old sick man: blind with the
Shadow of death on my face and my hands to lead me:
And he not ignorant: not sick —
                              but I

Fought in those battles! These were my own deeds!
These names he writes of mouthing them out as a man
          would
Names in Herodotus — dead and their wars to read —

These were my friends: these dead my companions:
I: Bernál Díaz: called del Castíllo:
Called in the time of my first fights El Galán:

I here in the turn of the day in the feel of
Darkness to come now: moving my chair with the
        change:
Thinking too much these times how the doves would
        wheel at

Evening over my youth and the air's strangeness:
Thinking too much of my old town of Medina
And the Spanish dust and the smell of the true rain:

I: poor: blind in the sun: I have seen
With these eyes those battles: I saw Montezúma:
I saw the armies of Mexico marching the leaning

Wind in their garments: the painted faces: the plumes
Blown on the light air: I saw that city:
I walked at night on those stones: in the shadowy rooms

I have heard the chink of my heel and the bats
        twittering:
I: poor as I am: I was young in that country:
These words were my life: these letters written

Cold on the page with the split ink and the shunt of the
Stubborn thumb: these marks at my fingers:
These are the shape of my own life . . .
                                and I hunted the

Unknown birds in the west with their beautiful wings!

Before, though, Paris was wonderful. Wanderers
Talking in all tongues from every country.
Fame was what they wanted in that town.
Fame could be found there too — flushed like quail
    in the
Cool dawn — struck among statues
Naked in hawthorn in the silver light.
James Joyce found it. Dublin bore him.
Could have sung with McCormack! Could he? He could.
Did he? He didn't. He walked by the winding Seine.
And what did he eat? He ate orts: oddities:
Oh he was poor: obscure: no one had heard of him:
Rolled on the floor on the floor with the pain in his eyes.
And found fame? He did. Ulysses: Yule Book:
Published to every people even in Erse.
(Molly Molly why did you say so Molly!)
Or the lad in the Rue de Notre Dame des Champs
At the carpenter's loft on the left-hand side going down —
The lad with the supple look like a sleepy panther —
And what became of him? Fame became of him.
Veteran out of the wars before he was twenty:
Famous at twenty-five: thirty a master —
Whittled a style for his time from a walnut stick
In a carpenter's loft in a street of that April city.

Where do they hang out now, the young ones, the
    wanderers,
Following fame by the rumor of praise in a town?
Where is fame in the world now? Where are the
    lovers of
Beauty of beauty that she moves among?

THE LEARNED MEN

Whose minds like horse or ox,
Dispassionate in the stall,
Grow great in girth and wax
Beyond the animal,

While mine, like country hog,
Grows leaner as I age,
Chivvied by flea and dog,
Baited by love and rage.

If mind by God was meant
To grow and gain in girth,
Swelling in sweet content,
I cease I have no worth:

But if it was God's will
That mind, no wish refused,
Should waste by wanting still
By God I am well used!

WHERE A POET'S FROM

Where he's born?
Settles? Where the papers claim him?
Carl Sandburg, born in Illinois,
died in Flat Rock, Carolina, in Chicago famous —

where was Sandburg from? Chicago?
People knew where Frost was from
in spite of San Francisco — from New England.
What town or what proud county knew this other
      coming?

He lived around: he lived in Kansas,
Chicago on the Old West Side,
Michigan, Nebraska — in Wisconsin.
Where was Carl from in the Carolinas when he died?

His tongue might tell: he talked "Peoria" —
O as in Oh or Low, the way
the railroad trainmen on the Illinois
called it in those cool reverberating stations.

His sound might say: he said "Missouri" —
a stumbled M and an S and an OO
long as a night freight off across the prairie
asking the moon for answers and the sound goes through
      and through.

Where was Sandburg from, old poet,
dead in Carolina in his great repute?
"Peoria," he said, "Missouri," the neglected names
that now, because his mouth has spoken them, are
      beautiful.

MARK'S SHEEP

Mark's sheep, I said, but they were only
stones, boulders in the uncropped grass,
granite shoulders weathered to the bone
and old as that first morning where God was.

And yet they looked like sheep — so like
you half expected them to startle,
bolt in a leap because some tyke
had barked, because a bluejay darted —

dart of shadow under blue of jay —
or someone shouted by the water trough,
slammed a car-door, drove away,
or squirrels quarreled, or a gun went off,

or just because they must: that terrified
impulse to be somewhere else
browsers and ruminators seem to share
as though they knew, they only, the sky falls

and *here* is dangerous (as of course it is).
But Mark's sheep never startled from the grass.
They knew their place, their boulders' business:
to let the nights go over, the days pass,

let years go, summer, autumn, winter,
each by itself, each motionless, alone,
praising the world by being in it,
praising the earth by being stone.

HEMINGWAY

"In some inexplicable way an accident."
                Mary Hemingway

Oh, not inexplicable. Death explains,
that kind of death: rewinds remembrance
backward like a film track till the laughing man
among the lilacs, peeling the green stem,
waits for the gunshot where the play began;

rewinds those Africas and Idahos and Spains
to find the table at the Closerie des Lilas,
sticky with syrup, where the flash of joy
flamed into blackness like that flash of steel.

The gun between the teeth explains,
The shattered mouth foretells the singing boy.

CUMMINGS

"He was sitting watching the sunset."
Marian Cummings, September 2, 1962

True
poet who could live and die
eye to eye

The rain ends, the sky slides
east a little as our skies here do
this time of year and lets the sunset through . . .

or not the sunset either but a blue
between the hill and what the cloud still hides
that promises
          a poet's blue

I should have known, my friend, you'd watch it too
eastward across New Hampshire where the night
found you in that glimpse of light

The cloud lifts and the rift of blue
blazes and the sun comes through

SKETCH FOR A PORTRAIT
OF MME G —— M ——

"Her room," you'd say — and wonder why you'd called it
Hers, as though she hadn't seven others
Not counting the reception room beside
The front door in red paper with a view
Of Paris in a bottle and real snow
Made out of something else and through the window
The railroad cutting where the trains went by
To Marly-le-château-du-roy: but somehow
Whether you came to dinner or to see
The last Picasso or because the sun
Blazed on her windows as you passed or just
Because you came, and whether she was there
Or down below in the garden or gone out
Or not come in yet, somehow when you came
You always crossed the hall and turned the doorknob
And went in; — "Her room" — as though the room
Itself were nearer her: as though the room
Were something she had left for you to see —
The room triangular with morning sunlight,
The room half-globed and low above the lamps,
The room oblique and leaning to the fire.
And yet it was not hers, not hers by title,
Nor hers because she'd had the walls redone
In rose to match the color of her dresses,
Nor hers because Le Bal du Comte Orgel
Lay on a chair and she had picked the flowers,
Nor merely hers because she lived in it.
No one, — not the most precisely careless

44

Distributor of household knick-knacks, boxes,
Candlesticks, pillows, receptables for ashes
Or photographs of children, — could have fixed
Its fine proportions in that attitude
Of gratified compliance worn by salons
Whose white-and-gold has settled into home;
And other men and women must have left
The touch of hands there — say, for one, old Gounod
Who'd written Mireille in the room and played
The airs from Baucis on the grand piano
And wasn't, you would understand, a man
To leave his mortal habitation empty
No matter how the doors had closed on him.
And yet you'd say, "Her room," as though you'd said
Her voice, Her manner, meaning something else
Than that she owned it; knowing it was not
A room to be possessed of, not a room
To give itself to people, not the kind
Of room you'd sit in and forget about,
Or sit in and look out from. It reserved
Something that in a woman you would call
Her reticence by which you'd mean her power
Of feeling what she had not put in words —
Which, in the room, was more perhaps the windows
And what there was beyond them that you saw
Only in shadows on the floor and ceiling
Than anything the room itself contained.
Sometimes toward twilight when the windows seemed
Faintly to let the half-light ebb away
And through that lapsing and last fall of day
The ancient dark a moment showed itself
And then was darkness — in that moment — then —
The room, made probable, made real, became

As strangely visible as if it were
The shape of something she was thinking of.

And there were afternoons when the snow fell
Softly across the wind and in the mirrors
The snow fell softly, flake on flake, the vague
Reflected falling in the long dim mirrors,
Faint snow across the image of the wind, —
And there were afternoons when the room remembered,
When her life passed in the mirrors of the room.

THE BOATMEN OF SANTORIN

The boatmen on the bay of Santorin
where the world blew up about the time of Minos
sit with their hands on their oars inviting the tourists.

Visit the myth! Visit the fable!
Visit the drowned volcano where the world
blew up about the time of Minos!

The sea sings. The sun shines.
Visit the end of the world! they shout at you.

And all at once on the bright blue
tourist sea, suds of pumice,
floating shoals of grey decaying stone,
grate at the wooden oars.

                    We float here
feathering death at our oar-blades.

46

CHARTRES

I do not wonder, stones,
You have withstood so long
The strong wind and the snows.

Were you not built to bear
The winter and the wind
That blows on the hill here?

But you have borne so long
Our eyes, our mortal eyes,
And are not worn —

BAHAMAS

Down there in those islands
Vines color of calico
Climb on the coral walls.
The surf falls in flowers.

Down there in those islands
Noon odor of indolence
Sleeps in the naked wind
In the wall's shadow.

Love is by day in those islands.
Love languor of Negresses

47

Lies in the shuttered rooms:
The blinds tremble.

Love is by day in those islands:
Nights, the slow tread of the sea
Tramples the scent and the flowers,
Stands in the stillness.

Night is the sea in those islands.
The lamp goes out on the balcony,
The leaf returns to its silence,
The sea to the reef.

Down there in those islands
Night is the sound of forever,
Night is the salt on the mouth,
Night is the sea.

BOY IN THE ROMAN ZOO

TO THE FLAMINGOS
                        Ravished arms,
delighted eyes — and all the rest,
parental cautions and alarms,
treacherous sidewalks and his best
blue suit forgotten. He has seen
heaven upon the further shore
and nothing in the null between
has mere existence anymore.

Those shapes of rose, those coals of ice,
command him as love never has
and only they can now suffice.
Forgotten is the child he was,
unguessed the man he will be. One
moment, free of both, he'll run
toward the flamingos in the sun.

WHERE THE HAYFIELDS WERE

Coming down the mountain in the twilight —
April it was and quiet in the air —
I saw an old man and his little daughter
Burning the meadows where the hayfields were.

Forksful of flame he scattered in the meadows.
Sparkles of fire in the quiet air
Burned in their circles and the silver flowers
Danced like candles where the hayfields were, —

Danced as she did in enchanted circles,
Curtseyed and danced along the quiet air:
Slightly she danced in the stillness, in the twilight,
Dancing in the meadows where the hayfields were.

THE SIGNAL

Why do they ring that bell
Twelve times in the steeple?

To say the hill has swung —
Houses and church and people,
All of them fast asleep —
To this place in time where the bell
Tilts to its iron tongue
Twelve times in the steeple.

Houses and hill don't care
Nor sleepers fast asleep.

But the steeple says to the star:
Here in the night we are,
Hill and houses and men.
Andromeda's shivering light,
Orion's distant flare,
Here we are in the night,
Here we go by again.
We go by you again says the bell,
Again, says the bell, again . . .

SPRING IN THESE HILLS

Slow May
deliberate in the peach tree,
lighting the pear blossoms, one first then another,
sullen almost sometimes,
comes,
delicately through the thaws of snow
to scatter
daffodils like drifting flaws
of sunlight on these winter hills.

THE OLD MAN TO THE LIZARD

Lizard, lover of heat, of high
Noon, of the hot stone, the golden
Sun in your unblinking eye —
And they say you are old, lizard, older than

Rocks you run on with those delicate
Fishbone fingers, skittering over
Ovens even cricket in his shell
Could never sing in — tell me, lover of

Sun, lover of noon, lizard,
Is it because the sun is gold with
Flame you love it so? Or is
Your love because your blood is cold?

CAPTIVITY
OF THE FLY

The fly against the window pane
That flings itself in flightless flight,
So it loves light,
Will die of love and die in vain.

Prisoner of the open wall
Where freedom is but turning round,
Still is it bound:
Love barred, there is no way at all.

My heart against the hard rib bone
Beat like a fly and would not be:
It had gone free
But that the shining world so shone.

LOVE
AND NOT

MY NAKED AUNT

Who puts off shift
Has love's concealment left.

Who puts off skin
Has pain to wind her in.

Who puts off flesh
Wears soul's enormous wish.

Who puts off bone

Has all of death for gown.

None go naked who have drawn this breath
Till love's put off and pain and wish and death.

WHAT ANY LOVER LEARNS

Water is heavy silver over stone.
Water is heavy silver over stone's
Refusal. It does not fall. It fills. It flows
Every crevice, every fault of the stone,
Every hollow. River does not run:
River presses its heavy silver self
Down into stone and stone refuses.

                              What runs,
Swirling and leaping into sun, is stone's
Refusal of the river, not the river.

YOU ALSO,
GAIUS VALERIUS CATULLUS

Fat-kneed god! Feeder of mangy leopards!
You who brought me into that one's bed
Whose breath is sweeter than a grass-fed heifer —
If *you* had not willed it, I had not willed it —
You who dumped me like a sack of milt
Limp in her eager taking arms as though
Her breast were no more than a bench to lie on,
Listen! Muncher of the pale-pipped apples!
Keeper of paunchy house-cats! Boozy god!
Dump me where you please, but not hereafter
Where the dawn has that *particular* laughter.

BROKEN PROMISE

That was by the door.
Leafy evening in the apple trees.
And you would not forget this anymore.
And even if you died there would be these

Touchings remembered.
                    And you would return
From any bourne from any shore
To find the evening in these leaves —
To find my arms beside this door . . .

I think, O, my not now Ophelia,
There are not always (like a moon)
Rememberings afterward:
                                        I think there are
Sometimes a few strange stars upon the sky.

STARVED LOVERS

Chrysanthemums last too long for these ravenous ladies
The flowers they prefer are brief, unfold
At evening filling the cool room then fade,
Budded at pleasure and at pleasure old.

Chrysanthemums stand too still for these starved ladies.
Staring like Vincent's sunlight, bright and still,
They burn until these feasters are afraid
Hunger may leave them and their lives be filled.

The ravenous ladies in the still-starved lives
Strip off the ever-burning leaves with silver knives.

NOVELLA

from *The Woman on the Stair*

(1)

THE WHITE POEM

With haste, with the haggard color,
With shad-blow, plum-blossoms (multitudes)
Came and again spring,
Sole on a bush, single in
Apple branches, tasteless,
Filling the low places as
Water in flood fills them:
Leaving blossomless hills.

Over were three gulls
And the oak making little cover,
And you were ashamed of love
Lacking the sheet, looking up
Mile after mile in the cup of the
Open sky and the birds in it —
Candle lacking and words.

Over were three gulls
And your mouth like salt and you hated me.
Why? For the winter's wait? —
For the haste? For the haggard color?

(2)

THE ABSENCE

Hunger nor thirst nor any bodily famine
Failing bread to be eaten, meat consumed,

Is comparable or any way to be likened to

This, this lack, this absence, this not to be found
Of you whom neither may tongue take nor fingers
Break to be broken nor the mouth devour —

Only by hands arms starved be with
Momentarily taking nothing away
But the need to return to you taking nothing **away.**

No hunger was ever sharp as this hunger —
The absence of you on a plain bed in this city
Counting the night out by the iron tongues.

(3)

THE TREACHERY

As a candle flame is straight within the curve of hands
So strictly stands

That moment in the violence of the snow.
Although the wind could blow,

Although the white unable wandering of the air
Whirled everywhere,

Although the storm drove wildly through the winter
    street,
The unnamed sudden doubt of her deceit

Stood in that violence like a breathless flame.
Where wildest winter came

There stood as still as candle to the palm
The desperate heart's inexplicable calm.

(4)
The Quarrel

I never said that you were changed.
I said — and if I looked at you
With fear it was my natural heart —
I said dear love that you were true.

I said your body was still yours
And bore no bruise where he had been:
Your mouth was still the mouth I knew,
The hair was yours, the throat, the skin.

I said I could not see his eyes
In your eyes doubled: could not hear
The whisper of his actual breath
Beneath your hair, against your ear.

I never said that you were changed:
I said — in dread as though you came
Unaltered from the earth of death —
I said your eyes were still the same!

(5)
The Reconciliation

Time like the repetitions of a child's piano
Brings me the room again the shallow lamp the love
The night the silence the slow bell the echoed answer.

By no thing here or lacking can the eyes discover
The hundred winter evenings that have gone between
Nor know for sure the night is this and not that other.

The room is here, the lamp is here, the mirror's leaning
Searches the same deep shadow where her knees are
    caught:
All these are here within the room as I have seen them.

Time has restored them all as in that rainy autumn:
Even the echoes of that night return to this —
All as they were when first the earthy evening brought
    them.

Between this night and that there is no human distance:
There is no space an arm could not out-reach by much —
And yet the stars most far apart are not more distant.

Between my hand that touched and her soft breast that
    touches
The irremediable past, as steep as stone,
Wider than water, like all land and ocean stretches:

We touch and by that touching farness are alone.

(6)
The Second Love

In love not love there never are two lovers:
There are but two together with blind eyes
Watching within what ecstasy love suffers.

One, like a shore at which the water rises,
Senses the flooding of a sea to spate
Her naked and lovely longing with its rising.

One, like the flooding of a sea, awaits
The smooth resistance of the gradual shore

To be fallen in shudder of hush from his headlong
    greatness.

What they remember each of the other more than
Meeting of mouths or even the profound touch
Is their own ecstasy heavy to be borne.

So it is, even with these whose touching
Makes them a moment on a bed to share
What time with all its timid gifts begrudges.

Neither her serious mouth nor pitiful hair
Nor his mouth mortal with the murderous need
Troubles their hearts to tenderness.

                        They stare
Each in the other's face like those who feed
Delight in mirrors: and as though alone
Learn from each other where their love will lead them.

(7)
THE ROOM BY THE RIVER

They think in each other's arms of the sound of the surf.
(The sound in that street is of barges:
The wake v's out, curves,
Breaks on the bulkhead blurring the water stars.)

They think how the sound of the surf is the sound of
    forever
Turning upon the returning of time,
Bringing the wave back that has left them,
Taking their knees again with the sea's climbing.

(The sound in that street is the sound of the barges:

One wave breaks along the brackish shore:
Nothing returns . . .)
                                    He rises from her arms to
Dress in silence and go out the door.

(8)

THE REMEMBRANCE

I have forgotten you. There is grey light on my
Hands and I have forgotten you. There is light enough.
There is light enough left to forget your face by,
Voice by, to forget you. As long as the
Light lasts on my hands I forget you.
There needs be some light: a little.
A man remembers by night — even the
Windows barely a sure shape and the
Shadows anything, standing for anything.
Night is never alone, it remembers.
At night the hair mouth eyes —
The eyes — at night they return to us.

Between the night and me this light,
Little enough, a thin cover,
Fragile defense against the meaning dark
Where eyes are always but not seen till night comes.
Now for a little there is light between.

(9)

THE LATE MEETING

Too cold too windy and too dark
The autumn dawn withholds the bees

64

And bold among the door-yard trees
The crow cries, the wild foxes bark.

Day alters, seasons alter, we
Walking the wet rut alter too:
The fault of strangeness is with you:
Strangeness is the fault in me.

We know each other, not the friend
Each for the other's love once made:
We know the cold, and are afraid
Of new years, now the year will end.

(10)

THE RELEASE

I know where time has departed:
Time has departed thither.
From that unaltering country
Never will time return.

Tawny and still is that country.
Thither is time gone.
Even the air is motionless:
No leaf may fall there.

Time has left me and gone
To that changeless and unchanged country.
Thither has time departed.
There at a day it stands.

You who stand in that country
You may not ruffle your hair:
You may not move nor may even
The scarf slip from you carelessly.

You are caught in the standing of time.
You may not move nor be changed.
Time's past is still:
Time's stillness has taken you.

This is the winter of time:
This is the water frozen:
The oak mute in the wind:
Love's memory motionless.

WINTER IS ANOTHER COUNTRY

If the autumn would
End! If the sweet season,
The late light in the tall trees, would
End! If the fragrance, the odor of
Fallen apples, dust on the road,
Water somewhere near, the scent of
Water touching me; if this would end
I could endure the absence in the night,
The hands beyond the reach of hands, the name
Called out and never answered with my name:
The image seen but never seen with sight.
I could endure this all
If autumn ended and the cold light came.

VOYAGE WEST

There was a time for discoveries —
For the headlands looming above in the
First light and the surf and the
Crying of gulls: for the curve of the
Coast north into secrecy.

That time is past.
The last lands have been peopled.
The oceans are known now.

Señora: once the maps have all been made
A man were better dead than find new continents.

A man would better never have been born
Than find upon the open ocean flowers
Drifted from islands where there are no islands,

Or midnight, out of sight of any land,
Smell on the altering air the odor of rosemary.

No fortune passes that misfortune —

To lift along the evening of the sky,
Certain as sun and sea, a new-found land
Steep from an ocean where no landfall can be.

MEMORY GREEN

Yes and when the warm unseasonable weather
Comes at the year's end of the next late year
And the southwest wind that smells of rain and summer
Strips the huge branches of their dying leaves,

And you at dusk along the Friedrichstrasse
Or you in Paris on the windy *quai*
Shuffle the shallow fallen leaves before you
Thinking the thoughts that like the grey clouds change,

You will not understand why suddenly sweetness
Fills in your heart or the tears come to your eyes:
You will stand in the June-warm wind and the leaves
    falling:
When was it so before, you will say, With whom?

You will not remember this at all: you will stand there
Feeling the wind on your throat, the wind in your sleeves,
You will smell the dead leaves in the grass of a garden:
You will close your eyes: With whom, you will say,
                              Ah where?

"NOT MARBLE NOR THE GILDED MONUMENTS"

for Adele

The praisers of women in their proud and beautiful
    poems,
Naming the grave mouth and the hair and the eyes,
Boasted those they loved should be forever remembered:
These were lies.

The words sound but the face in the Istrian sun is
    forgotten.
The poet speaks but to her dead ears no more.
The sleek throat is gone — and the breast that was
    troubled to listen:
Shadow from door.

Therefore I will not praise your knees nor your fine
    walking
Telling you men shall remember your name as long
As lips move or breath is spent or the iron of English
Rings from a tongue.

I shall say you were young, and your arms straight, and
    your mouth scarlet:
I shall say you will die and none will remember you:
Your arms change, and none remember the swish of your
    garments,
Nor the click of your shoe.

Not with my hand's strength, not with difficult labor

Springing the obstinate words to the bones of your breast
And the stubborn line to your young stride and the
        breath to your breathing
And the beat to your haste
Shall I prevail on the hearts of unborn men to remember.

(What is a dead girl but a shadowy ghost
Or a dead man's voice but a distant and vain affirmation
Like dream words most)

Therefore I will not speak of the undying glory of
        women.
I will say you were young and straight and your skin fair
And you stood in the door and the sun was a shadow of
        leaves on your shoulders
And a leaf on your hair —

I will not speak of the famous beauty of dead women:
I will say the shape of a leaf lay once on your hair.
Till the world ends and the eyes are out and the mouths
        broken
Look!
        It is there.

UNFINISHED HISTORY

We have loved each other in this time twenty years
And with such love as few men have in them even for
One or for the marriage month or the hearing of

Three nights' carts in the street but it will leave them.
We have been lovers the twentieth year now:
Our bed has been made in many houses and evenings.

The apple-tree moves at the window in this house:
There were palms rattled the night through in one,
In one there were red tiles and the sea's hours.

We have made our bed in the changes of many
    months —
The light of the day is still overlong in the windows
Till night shall bring us the lamp and one another.

Those that have seen her have no thought what she is:
Her face is clear in the sun as a palmful of water.
Only by night and in love are the dark winds on it . . .

I wrote this poem that day when I thought
Since we have loved we two so long together
Shall we have done together — all love gone?

Or how then will it be with us when the breath
Is no more able for such joy and the blood is
Thin in the throat and the time not come for death?

POEM IN PROSE

This poem is for my wife.
I have made it plainly and honestly:
The mark is on it
Like the burl on the knife.

I have not made it for praise.
She has no more need for praise
Than summer has
Or the bright days.

In all that becomes a woman
Her words and her ways are beautiful:
Love's lovely duty,
The well-swept room.

Wherever she is there is sun
And time and a sweet air:
Peace is there,
Work done.

There are always curtains and flowers
And candles and baked bread
And a cloth spread
And a clean house.

Her voice when she sings is a voice
At dawn by a freshening sea
Where the wave leaps in the
Wind and rejoices.

Wherever she is it is now.
It is here where the apples are:

Here in the stars,
In the quick hour.

The greatest and richest good,
My own life to live in,
This she has given me —

If giver could.

EVER SINCE

What do you remember thinking back?
What do you think of at dusk in the slack
Evening when the mind refills
With the cool past as a well fills in
Darkness from forgotten rains?

Do you think of waking in the all-night train,
The curtains drawn, the Mediterranean
Blue, blue, and the sellers of oranges
Holding heaped up morning toward you?

Do you think of Kumomoto-Ken
And the clogs going by in the night and the scent of
Clean mats, the sound of the peepers,
The wind in the pines, the dark sleep?

Do you think how Santiago stands at
Night under its stars, under its Andes:

Its bells like heavy birds that climb
Widening circles out of time?

I saw them too. I know those places.
There are no mountains — scarcely a face
Of all the faces you have seen,
Or a town or a room, but I have seen it.

Even at dusk in the deep chair
Letting the long past take you, bear you —
Even then you never leave me, never can.
Your eyes close, your small hands
Keep their secrets in your lap:
Wherever you are we two were happy.

I wonder what those changing lovers do,
Watching each other in the darkening room,
Whose world together is the night they've shared:
Whose past is parting: strangers side by side.

LATE ABED

Ah, but a good wife!
To lie late in a warm bed
(warm where she was) with your life
suspended like a music in the head,
hearing her foot in the house, her broom
on the pine floor of the down-stairs room,
hearing the window toward the sun go up,
the tap turned on, the tap turned off,
the saucer clatter to the coffee cup . . .

To lie late in the odor of coffee
thinking of nothing at all, listening . . .

and she moves here, she moves there,
and your mouth hurts still where last she kissed you:
you think how she looked as she left, the bare
thigh, and went to her adorning . . .

You lie there listening and she moves —
prepares her house to hold another morning,
prepares another day to hold her loves . . .

You lie there
thinking of nothing
watching the sky . . .

HOTEL BREAKFAST

On a stale morning
in a miserable winter town in Illinois
neither of us ever heard of,

sipping a sticky cup of some
(not tea, not coffee, cocoa?) tepid brew
you surely, of all living, never knew,

the napkin reeking of its dead cigars
(scent of yellow roses was your warning),
suddenly,
       across the table,
             you.

The plastic prisms of the chandelier
shiver with laughter from another year,
another country, Oh, another life;
the cold sun crawls along the butter knife.

I tremble, heartsick with a mortal fear —

What brings you here?

CALYPSO'S ISLAND

I know very well, goddess, she is not beautiful
As you are: could not be. She is a woman,
Mortal, subject to the chances: duty of

Childbed, sorrow that changes cheeks, the tomb —
For unlike you she will grow grey, grow older,
Grey and older, sleep in that small room.

She is not beautiful as you, O golden!
You are immortal and will never change
And can make me immortal also, fold

Your garment round me, make me whole and strange
As those who live forever, not the while
That we live, keep me from those dogging dangers —

Ships and the wars — in this green, far-off island,
Silent of all but sea's eternal sound
Or sea-pine's when the lull of surf is silent.

Goddess, I know how excellent this ground,
What charmed contentment of the removed heart
The bees make in the lavender where pounding

Surf sounds far off and the bird that darts
Darts through its own eternity of light,
Motionless in motion, and the startled

Hare is startled into stone, the fly
Forever golden in the flickering glance
Of leafy sunlight that still holds it. I

Know you, goddess, and your caves that answer
Ocean's confused voices with a voice:
Your poplars where the storms are turned to dances;

Arms where the heart is turned. You give the choice
To hold forever what forever passes,
To hide from what will pass, forever. Moist,

Moist are your well-stones, goddess, cool your grasses!
And she — she is a woman with that fault
Of change that will be death in her at last!

Nevertheless I long for the cold, salt,
Restless, contending sea and for the island
Where the grass dies and the seasons alter:

Where that one wears the sunlight for a while.

"THE WILD OLD WICKED MAN"

Too old for love and still to love! —
Yeats's predicament and mine — all men's:
the aging Adam who must strut and shove
and caper his obscene pretense . . .

And yet, within the dry thorn grove,
singer to singer in the dusk, there cries
(Listen! Ah, listen, the wood dove!)
something conclusion never satisfies;

and still when day ends and the wind goes down
and not a tree stirs, not a leaf,
some passion in the sea beats on
and on . . .
           (Oh, listen, the sea reef!)

Too old for love and still to long . . .
for what? For one more flattering proof
the flesh lives and the beast is strong? —
once more upon the pulse that hammering hoof?

Or is there something the persistent dove,
the ceaseless surges and the old man's lust
all know and cannot say? Is love

what nothing concludes, nothing must —
pure certainty?

          And does the passionate man
most nearly know it when no passion can?
Is this the old man's triumph, to pursue
impossibility — and take it too?

"STRANGE THING . . . TO BE AN AMERICAN"

MY SKY, MY MOUNTAIN

from American Letter
for Gerald Murphy

The wind is east but the hot weather continues,
Blue and no clouds, the sound of the leaves thin,
Dry like the rustling of paper, scored across
With the slate-shrill screech of the locusts.
                                    The tossing of
Pines is the low sound. In the wind's running
The wild carrots smell of the burning sun.

Why should I think of the dolphins at Capo di Mele?
Why should I see in my mind the taut sail
And the hill over St.-Tropez and your hand on the tiller?
Why should my heart be troubled with palms still?
I am neither a sold boy nor a Chinese official
Sent to sicken in Pa for some Lo-Yang dish.
This is my own land, my sky, my mountain:
This — not the humming pines and the surf and the
    sound
At the Ferme Blanche, nor Port Cros in the dusk and
    the harbor
Floating the motionless ship and the sea-drowned star.
I am neither Po Chü-i nor another after
Far from home, in a strange land, daft
For the talk of his own sort and the taste of his lettuces.
This land is my native land. And yet
I am sick for home for the red roofs and the olives,
And the foreign words and the smell of the sea fall.
How can a wise man have two countries?
How can a man have the earth and the wind and want
A land far off, alien — silence of palm trees
And the yellow gorse at noon in the long calms?

It is a strange thing to be an American.
It is strange to live on the high world in the stare
Of the naked sun and the stars as our bones live.
Men in the old lands housed by their rivers.
They built their towns in the vales in the earth's shelter.
We first inhabit the world. We dwell
On the half earth, on the open curve of a continent.
Sea is divided from sea by the day-fall. The dawn
Rides the low east with us many hours;
First are the capes, then are the shorelands, now

The blue Appalachians faint at the day rise;
The willows shudder with light on the long Ohio:
The Lakes scatter the low sun: the prairies
Slide out of dark: in the eddy of clean air
The smoke goes up from the high plains of Wyoming:
The steep Sierras arise: the struck foam
Flames at the wind's heel on the far Pacific.
Already the noon leans to the eastern cliff:
The elms darken the door and the dust-heavy lilacs.

This, this is our land, this is our people,
This that is neither a land nor a race. We must reap
The wind here in the grass for our soul's harvest:
Here we must eat our salt or our bones starve.
Here we must live or live only as shadows.
This is our race, we that have none, that have had
Neither the old walls nor the voices around us,
This is our land, this is our ancient ground —
The new earth, the mixed bloods and the strangers,
The different eyes, the wind, and the heart's change.
This our country-earth, our blood, our kind.
Here we will live our years till the earth blind us —

The wind blows from the east. The leaves fall.
Far off in the pines a jay rises.
The wind smells of haze and the wild ripe apples.

I think of the masts at Cette and the sweet rain.

GEOGRAPHY OF THE NEW WORLD

from *America Was Promises*

Who is the voyager in these leaves?
Who is the traveler in this journey
Deciphers the revolving night: receives
The signal from the light returning?

America was promises to whom?
                              East were the
Dead kings and the remembered sepulchres:
West was the grass.
            The groves of the oaks were at evening.

Eastward are the nights where we have slept.

And we move on: we move down:
With the first light we push forward:
We descend from the past as a wandering people from
        mountains.
We cross into the day to be discovered.

The dead are left where they fall — at dark
At night late under the coverlets.
We mark the place with the shape of our teeth on our
        fingers.
The room is left as it was: the love

Who is the traveler in these leaves these
Annual waters and beside the doors
Jonquils: then the rose: the eaves

Heaping the thunder up: the mornings
Opening on like great valleys
Never till now approached: the familiar trees
Far off, distant with the future:
The hollyhocks beyond the afternoons:
The butterflies over the ripening fruit on the balconies:
And all beautiful
All before us

America was always promises.
From the first voyage and the first ship there were
     promises —
"the tropic bird which does not sleep at sea"
"the great mass of dark heavy clouds which is a sign"
"the drizzle of rain without wind which is a sure sign"
"the whale which is an indication"
"the stick appearing to be carved with iron"
"the stalk loaded with roseberries"
"and all these signs were from the west"
"and all night heard birds passing."

Who is the voyager on these coasts?
Who is the traveler in these waters
Expects the future as a shore: foresees
Like Indies to the west the ending — he
The rumor of the surf intends?

America was promises — to whom?

And the child says I see the lightning on you.

The weed between the railroad tracks
Tasting of sweat: tasting of poverty:

The bitter and pure taste where the hawk hovers:
Native as the deer bone in the sand

O my America for whom?

For whom the promises? For whom the river
"It flows west! Look at the ripple of it!"
The grass "So that it was wonderful to see
And endless without end with wind wonderful!"
The Great Lakes: landless as oceans: their beaches
Coarse sand: clean gravel: pebbles:
Their bluffs smelling of sunflowers: smelling of surf:
Of fresh water: of wild sunflowers . . . wilderness.
For whom the evening mountains toward the sky:
The night wind from the west: the moon descending?

Never before: never in any summer:
Never were days so generous: stars so mild:
Even in old men's talk or in books or remembering
Far back to a gone childhood
Or farther still to the light where Homer wanders —
The air all lucid with the solemn blue
That hills take at the distance beyond change . . .
That time takes also at the distances.

Never were there promises as now:
Never was green deeper: earth warmer:
Light more beautiful to see: the sound of
Water lovelier: the many forms of
Leaves: stones: clouds: beasts: shadows
Clearer more admirable or the faces
More like answering faces or the hands
Quicker: more brotherly:

                        the aching taste of
Time more salt upon the tongue: more human

Never in any summer: and to whom?

Listen! Brothers! Generation!
Companions of leaves: of the sun: of the slow evenings:
Companions of the many days: of all of them:
Listen! Believe the speaking dead! Believe
The journey is our journey. Oh believe
The signals were to us: the signs: the birds by
Night: the breaking surf.

                    Believe

America is promises to
Take!
America is promises to
Us
To take them
Brutally
With love but
Take them.

Oh believe this!

1933

"The first I knew was the spirit of my fellow, Elpenor, whose body was not yet interred under the ample ground. We had left him unwept and unburied in the halls of Circe, for that these other labors came upon us urgently. When I saw him I had compassion and sharply cried across to him: 'Elpenor, how come you here into the gloomy shades? Your feet have been quicker than my ship.' He . . . answered me":

From Book XI of *The Odyssey*
(Lawrence's translation)

It is I, Odysseus — Elpenor —
Oarsman: death is between us.

Three days I have waited you,
Coming my own way,
Not your way,

(The oar-handle hard to the nipple):
Not being come in the ship,

Neither by dry earth,
There being no dry earth,

But roundabout by an art:
By the deft-in-air-darting

Way of an art severing
Earth or air or whatever.

And the place I believe to be Hell from the
Many dead and the pelts of

Great captains, emperors,
Princes, leaders-of-men,

Their rumps turned round to the wind,
And the rich with their eyes hidden,

And the redblooded, twofisted, gogetting,
He-ghosts froghonking wretchedly,

And from cairns and from creeks and from rock piles,
And out of the holes of foxes,

Fools booming like oracles,
Philosophers promising more

And worse to come of it yet
And proving it out of the textbooks.

Also the young men
Their rears strung out on the fences

Watching for shifts in the breeze:
And beyond under the lee the

Actual dead: the millions
Only a god could have killed.

The place I believe to be Hell from the
Cold and the cries and the welter of

Kings, dukes, dictators,
Heroes, headmen of cities,

Ranting orations from balconies,
Boasting to lead us back to the

Other days: to the odor of
Cooked leeks in the cold and our

Wives and the well-known landmarks —
To the normal life of a man as in

Old time and in sun,
The noon's work done

And the butterflies in their pairs
Under the beams of the areas.

*

Is it to these shores,
Odysseus, contriver of horses,
You, of all men born,

Come, and alive, demanding
The way back to your land? —
The way back to the sands and the

Boat-grooved beaches of years
Before the war and the spear-handling?

Wishful still to return
Do you ask way by the earth

Or by dark sea to a country
Known under other suns?

Roads on the sea fade,
And only the old ladies

Remembering scarlet coats
Hope to return to the lotuses.

Let tit-formed Tiresias tell you,
Tasting the bloody helm,
The way back by the bell or the

Book or the wars or the envy of
Men aroused against men
With a Heaven-on-earth at the end of it!

For myself — if you ask me —
There's no way back over sea water,

Nor by earth's oaks, nor beyond them:
There is only the way on.

You had best, trusting neither to
Charts nor to prophets but seamanship,
Take to the open sea,

Till you come to a clean place
With the smell of the pine in your faces and

Broom and a bitter turf
And the larks blown over the surf and the

Rocks red to the wave-height:
No sound but the wave's:

No call of a cock from the
Windward shore nor of oxen —

Gull's shadow for hawk's,
Gull's cry for the hawk's cry —

Take to the open sea
And head for the star at evening,

For an unplowed country,
Pure under cleansing sun,

With the dung burned dry on the gravel
And only the sand to have,

And begin it again: start over,
Forgetting the raised loaves and the

Home cows and the larders of
Sweating stone — the arms of the

Girl you left under lamb-skins: —
Begin it again with the hammer of

Hard rain on your heads and the
Raw fern for your bedding and

Thirst and the sea-cow's cough,
Lifting your smoke aloft
In spite of gods and the prophecy!

You have only to cross this place
And launch ship and get way on her

Working her out with the oars to the
Full wind and go forward and

94

Bring yourselves to a home:
To a new land: to an ocean

Never sailed. Not to Ithaca,
Not to your beds — but the withering

Seaweed under the thorn and the
Gulls and another morning . . .

*

As long as you bury me there on the beach
With my own oar stuck in the sand
So that ships standing along in
May see the stick of it straighter (though grey) than the
Olives, and ease all, and say —
"There is some man dead there that once pulled
"Water as we do with these and the thing is his
"Oarsweep" . . .
    As long as you bury me there
What will it matter to me if my name
Lacks, and the fat-leaved beach-plants cover my
Mound, and the wood of the oars goes silver as
Drift sea wood goes silver . . .

SPEECH TO THOSE WHO
SAY COMRADE

The brotherhood is not by the blood certainly,
But neither are men brothers by speech — by saying so:
Men are brothers by life lived and are hurt for it.

Hunger and hurt are the great begetters of brotherhood:
Humiliation has gotten much love:
Danger I say is the nobler father and mother.

Those are as brothers whose bodies have shared fear
Or shared harm or shared hurt or indignity.
Why are the old soldiers brothers and nearest?

For this: with their minds they go over the sea a little
And find themselves in their youth again as they were in
Soissons and Meaux and at Ypres and those cities:

A French loaf and the girls with their eyelids painted
Bring back to aging and lonely men
Their twentieth year and the metal odor of danger.

It is this in life which of all things is tenderest —
To remember together with unknown men the days
Common also to them and perils ended:

It is this which makes of many a generation —
A wave of men who having the same years
Have in common the same dead and the changes.

The solitary and unshared experience

Dies of itself like the violations of love
Or lives on as the dead live eerily:

The unshared and single man must cover his
Loneliness as a girl her shame for the way of
Life is neither by one man nor by suffering.

Who are the born brothers in truth? The puddlers
Scorched by the same flame in the same foundries,
Those who have spat on the same boards with the blood
    in it,

Ridden the same rivers with green logs,
Fought the police in the parks of the same cities,
Grinned for the same blows, the same flogging,

Veterans out of the same ships, factories,
Expeditions for fame: the founders of continents:
Those that hid in Geneva a time back,

Those that have hidden and hunted and all such —
Fought together, labored together: they carry the
Common look like a card and they pass touching.

Brotherhood! No word said can make you brothers!
Brotherhood only the brave earn and by danger or
Harm or by bearing hurt and by no other.

Brotherhood here in the strange world is the rich and
Rarest giving of life and the most valued,
Not to be had for a word or a week's wishing.

SPEECH TO A CROWD

Tell me, my patient friends, awaiters of messages,
From what other shore, from what stranger,
Whence, was the word to come? Who was to lesson
    you?

Listeners under a child's crib in a manger,
Listeners once by the oracles, now by the transoms,
Whom are you waiting for? Who do you think will
    explain?

Listeners thousands of years and still no answer —
Writers at night to Miss Lonely-Hearts, awkward spellers,
Open your eyes! There is only earth and the man!

There is only you. There is no one else on the telephone:
No one else is on the air to whisper:
No one else but you will push the bell.

No one knows if you don't: neither ships
Nor landing-fields decode the dark between.
You have your eyes and what your eyes see, is.

The earth you see is really the earth you are seeing.
The sun is truly excellent, truly warm,
Women are beautiful as you have seen them —

Their breasts (believe it) like cooing of doves in a
    portico.
They bear at their breasts tenderness softly. Look at
    them!

Look at yourselves. You are strong. You are well formed.

Look at the world — the world you never took!
It is really true you may live in the world heedlessly.
Why do you wait to read it in a book then?

Write it yourselves! Write to yourselves if you need to!
Tell yourselves there is sun and the sun will rise.
Tell yourselves the earth has food to feed you.

Let the dead men say that men must die!
Who better than you can know what death is?
How can a bone or a broken body surmise it?

Let the dead shriek with their whispering breath.
Laugh at them! Say the murdered gods may wake
But we who work have end of work together.

Tell yourselves the earth is yours to take!

Waiting for messages out of the dark you were poor.
The world was always yours: you would not take it.

ILLUSTRATIONS

from *Frescoes for Mr. Rockefeller's City*

LANDSCAPE AS A NUDE

She lies on her left side her flank golden:
Her hair is burned black with the strong sun.
The scent of her hair is of rain in the dust on her
    shoulders:
She has brown breasts and the mouth of no other
    country.

Ah she is beautiful here in the sun where she lies:
She is not like the soft girls naked in vineyards
Nor the soft naked girls of the English islands
Where the rain comes in with the surf on an east wind:

Hers is the west wind and the sunlight: the west
Wind is the long clean wind of the continents —
The wind turning with earth, the wind descending
Steadily out of the evening and following on.

The wind here where she lies is west: the trees
Oak ironwood cottonwood hickory: standing in
Great groves they roll on the wind as the sea would.
The grasses of Iowa Illinois Indiana

Run with the plunge of the wind as a wave tumbling.

Under her knees there is no green lawn of the
    Florentines:
Under her dusty knees is the corn stubble:
Her belly is flecked with the flickering light of the corn.

She lies on her left side her flank golden:
Her hair is burned black with the strong sun.
The scent of her hair is of dust and of smoke on her
　　shoulders:
She has brown breasts and the mouth of no other
　　country.

WILDWEST*

There were none of my blood in this battle:
There were Minneconjous, Sans Arcs, Brules,
Many nations of Sioux: they were few men galloping.

This would have been in the long days in June:
They were galloping well deployed under the plum-trees:
They were driving riderless horses: themselves they were
　　few.

Crazy Horse had done it with few numbers.
Crazy Horse was small for a Lakota.
He was riding always alone thinking of something:

He was standing alone by the picket lines by the ropes:
He was young then, he was thirty when he died:
Unless there were children to talk he took no notice.

When the soldiers came for him there on the other side
On the Greasy Grass in the villages we were shouting
"Hoka Hey! Crazy Horse will be riding!"

They fought in the water: horses and men were
　　drowning:
They rode on the butte: dust settled in sunlight:
Hoka Hey! they lay on the bloody ground.

* Black Elk's memories of Crazy Horse recorded by Neihardt.

No one could tell of the dead which man was Custer . . .
That was the end of his luck: by that river.
The soldiers beat him at Slim Buttes once:

They beat him at Willow Creek when the snow lifted:
The last time they beat him was the Tongue.
He had only the meat he had made and of that little.

Do you ask why he should fight? It was his country:
My God should he not fight? It was his.
But after the Tongue there were no herds to be hunting:

He cut the knots of the tails and he led them in:
He cried out "I am Crazy Horse! Do not touch me!"
There were many soldiers between and the gun
    glinting . . .

And a Mister Josiah Perham of Maine had much of the
land Mister Perham was building the Northern Pacific
railroad that is Mister Perham was saying at lunch that

forty say fifty millions of acres in gift and
government grant outright ought to be worth a
wide price on the Board at two-fifty and

later a Mister Cooke had relieved Mister Perham and
later a Mister Morgan relieved Mister Cooke:
Mister Morgan converted at prices current:

It was all prices to them: they never looked at it:
why should they look at the land? they were Empire
    Builders:
it was all in the bid and the asked and the ink on their
    books . . .

When Crazy Horse was there by the Black Hills

His heart would be big with the love he had for that
    country
And all the game he had seen and the mares he had
    ridden

And how it went out from you wide and clean in the
    sunlight

BURYING GROUND BY THE TIES

Ayee! Ai! This is heavy earth on our shoulders:
There were none of us born to be buried in this earth:
Niggers we were, Portuguese, Magyars, Polacks:

We were born to another look of the sky certainly.
Now we lie here in the river pastures:
We lie in the mowings under the thick turf:

We hear the earth and the all-day rasp of the grass-
    hoppers.
It was we laid the steel to this land from ocean to
    ocean:
It was we (if you know) put the U. P. through the passes

Bringing her down into Laramie full load,
Eighteen mile on the granite anticlinal,
Forty-three foot to the mile and the grade holding:

It was we did it: hunkies of our kind.
It was we dug the caved-in holes for the cold water:
It was we built the gully spurs and the freight sidings:

Who would do it but we and the Irishmen bossing us?
It was all foreign-born men there were in this country:
It was Scotsmen, Englishmen, Chinese, Squareheads,
    Austrians . . .

Ayee! but there's weight to the earth under it.
Not for this did we come out — to be lying here
Nameless under the ties in the clay cuts:

There's nothing good in the world but the rich will
    buy it:
Everything sticks to the grease of a gold note —
Even a continent — even a new sky!

Do not pity us much for the strange grass over us:
We laid the steel to the stone stock of these mountains:
The place of our graves is marked by the telegraph poles!

It was not to lie in the bottoms we came out
And the trains going over us here in the dry hollows . . .

OIL PAINTING OF THE ARTIST AS THE ARTIST

The plump Mr. Pl'f is washing his hands of America:
The plump Mr. Pl'f is in ochre with such hair:

America is in blue-black-grey-green-sandcolor.
America is a continent — many lands:

The plump Mr. Pl'f is washing his hands of America.
He is pictured at Pau on the *place* and his eyes glaring:

He thinks of himself as an exile from all this,
As an émigré from his own time into history

(History being an empty house without owners
A practical man may get in by the privy stones:

The dead are excellent hosts, they have no objections,
And once in he can nail the knob on the next one

Living the life of a classic in bad air

With himself for the Past and his face in the glass for
    Posterity).

The Cinquecento is nothing at all like Nome
Or Natchez or Wounded Knee or the Shenandoah.

Your vulgarity, Tennessee: your violence, Texas:
The rocks under your fields, Ohio, Connecticut:

Your clay, Missouri, your clay: you have driven him out.
You have shadowed his life, Appalachians, purple
    mountains.

There is much too much of your flowing, Mississippi:
He prefers a tidier stream with a terrace for trippers and

Cypresses mentioned in Horace or Henry James:
He prefers a country where everything carries the name
    of a

Countess or real king or an actual palace or
Something in Prose and the stock prices all in Italian.

There is more shade for an artist under a fig
Than under the whole rock range (he finds) of the
    Big Horns.

EMPIRE BUILDERS

THE MUSEUM ATTENDANT:

This is *The Making of America in Five Panels*:

This is Mister Harriman making America:
Mister-Harriman-is-buying-the-Union-Pacific-at-Seventy:
The Santa Fe is shining on his hair.

This is Commodore Vanderbilt making America:
Mister-Vanderbilt-is-eliminating-the-short-interest-in-
    Hudson:
Observe the carving on the rocking chair.

This is J. P. Morgan making America:
(The Tennessee Coal is behind to the left of the Steel
    Company.)
Those in mauve are braces he is wearing.

This is Mister Mellon making America:
Mister-Mellon-is-represented-as-a-symbolical-figure-in
    aluminum-
Strewing-bank-stocks-on-a-burnished-stair.

This is the Bruce is the Barton making America:
Mister-Barton-is-selling-us-Doctor's-Deliciousest-Dentifrice.
This is he in beige with the canary.

You have just beheld the Makers making America:
This is The Making of America in Five Panels:
America lies to the west-southwest of the switch-tower:
There is nothing to see of America but land.

THE ORIGINAL DOCUMENT
UNDER THE PANEL PAINT:

"To Thos. Jefferson Esq. his obd't serv't
M. Lewis: captain: detached:
                                        Sir:

Having in mind your repeated commands in this matter,
And the worst half of it done and the streams mapped,

And we here on the back of this beach beholding the
Other ocean — two years gone and the cold

Breaking with rain for the third spring since St. Louis,
The crows at the fishbones on the frozen dunes,

The first cranes going over from south north,
And the river down by a mark of the pole since the
    morning,

And time near to return, and a ship (Spanish)
Lying in for the salmon: and fearing chance or the

Drought or the Sioux should deprive you of these
    discoveries —
Therefore we send by sea in this writing.

                    Above the
Platte there were long plains and a clay country:
Rim of the sky far off, grass under it,

Dung for the cook fires by the sulphur licks.
After that there were low hills and the sycamores,

And we poled up by the Great Bend in the skiffs:
The honey bees left us after the Osage River:

The wind was west in the evenings, and no dew and
    the
Morning Star larger and whiter than usual —

The winter rattling in the brittle haws.
The second year there was sage and the quail calling.

All that valley is good land by the river:
Three thousand miles and the clay cliffs and

Rue and beargrass by the water banks
And many birds and the brant going over and tracks of

Bear, elk, wolves, marten: the buffalo
Numberless so that the cloud of their dust covers them:

The antelope fording the fall creeks, and the mountains
    and
Grazing lands and the meadow lands and the ground

Sweet and open and well-drained.
                                        We advise you to
Settle troops at the forks and to issue licenses:

Many men will have living on these lands.
There is wealth in the earth for them all and the wood
    standing

And wild birds on the water where they sleep.
There is stone in the hills for the towns of a great
    people . . ."

You have just beheld the Makers Making America:

They screwed her scrawny and gaunt with their seven-
    year panics:
They bought her back on their mortgages old-whore-
    cheap:
They fattened their bonds at her breasts till the thin
    blood ran from them.

Men have forgotten how full clear and deep
The Yellowstone moved on the gravel and the grass
    grew
When the land lay waiting for her westward people!

BACKGROUND WITH REVOLUTIONARIES

And the corn singing Millennium!
Lenin! Millennium! Lennium!

When they're shunting the cars on the Katy a mile off
When they're shunting the cars when they're shunting
the cars on the Katy
You can hear the clank of the couplings riding away...

Also Comrade Devine who writes of America
Most instructively having in 'Seventy-four
Crossed to the Hoboken side on the Barclay Street Ferry.

She sits on a settle in the State of North Dakota,
O she sits on a settle in the State of North Dakota,
She can hear the engines whistle over Iowa and Idaho.

Also Comrade Edward Remington Ridge
Who has prayed God since the April of 'Seventeen
To replace in his life his lost (M.E.) religion.

And The New York Daily Worker *goes a'blowing over*
Arkansas,
The New York Daily Worker *goes a'blowing over*
Arkansas,
The grasses let it go along the Ozarks over Arkansas.

Even Comrade Grenadine Grilt who has tried since
August tenth for something to feel about strongly in
Verses — his personal passions having tired.

I can tell my land by the jays in the apple-trees,
Tell my land by the jays in the apple-trees,
I can tell my people by the blue-jays in the apple-trees.

109

Aindt you read in d' books you are all brudders?
D' glassic historic objective broves you are brudders!
You and d' Wops and d' Chinks you are all brudders!
Havend't you got it d' same ideology? Havend't you?

When it's yesterday in Oregon it's one A M in Maine
And she slides: and the day slides: and it runs: runs
> *over us:*
And the bells strike twelve strike twelve strike twelve
In Marblehead in Buffalo in Cheyenne in Cherokee:
Yesterday runs on the states like a crow's shadow.

For Marx has said to us, Workers what do you need?
And Stalin has said to us, Starvers what do you need?
You need the Dialectical Materialism!

She's a tough land under the corn, mister:
She has changed the bone in the cheeks of many races:
She has winced the eyes of the soft Slavs with her sun
> *on them:*

She has tried the fat from the round rumps of Italians:
Even the voice of the English has gone dry
And hard on the tongue and alive in the throat speaking.

She's a tough land under the oak-trees, mister:
It may be she can change the word in the book
As she changes the bone of a man's head in his children:
It may be that the earth and the men remain . . .

There is too much sun on the lids of my eyes to be
> *listening.*

BRAVE NEW WORLD

But you, Thomas Jefferson,
You could not lie so still,
You could not bear the weight of stone
On the quiet hill,

You could not keep your green grown peace
Nor hold your folded hand
If you could see your new world now,
Your new sweet land.

There was a time, Tom Jefferson,
When freedom made free men.
The new found earth and the new freed mind
Were brothers then.

There was a time when tyrants feared
The new world of the free.
Now freedom is afraid and shrieks
At tyranny.

Words have not changed their sense so soon
Nor tyranny grown new.
The truths you held, Tom Jefferson,
Will still hold true.

What's changed is freedom in this age.
What great men dared to choose
Small men now dare neither win
Nor lose.

Freedom, when men fear freedom's use
But love its useful name,
Has cause and cause enough for fear
And cause for shame.

We fought a war in freedom's name
And won it in our own.
We fought to free a world and raised
A wall of stone.

Your countrymen who could have built
The hill fires of the free
To set the dry world all ablaze
With liberty —

To burn the brutal thorn in Spain
Of bigotry and hate
And the dead lie and the brittle weed
Beyond the Plate:

Who could have heaped the bloody straw,
The dung of time, to light
The Danube in a sudden flame
Of hope by night —

Your countrymen who could have hurled
Their freedom like a brand
Have cupped it to a candle spark
In a frightened hand.

Freedom that was a thing to use
They've made a thing to save
And staked it in and fenced it round
Like a dead man's grave.

SHIP OF FOOLS

                  shoaled on this shingle,
Beached by the ebbed age, grounded . . .

If you want spectacles, WE are a spectacle!
The living lot, the generation,
Poking around in pools on the mudflat,
Kicking at clams, Cokes, condoms,
Dead fish, minute animalcula,
Ear cocked to the long, withdrawing
Gurgle out of a ketchup bottle
Sucked by the descending silt . . .

Where are the fountains of the deep, the fountains?
Where are the springs of the sea to enter them?

The ship fast and the fools everywhere!

Fools off in the muck to the eastward
Waiting for history to flood
On the date set by the Central Praesidium:
A tide in the affairs of men
Fixed by the water-works, a fraudulent
Season of the sea . . .

                      Fools
Off to the west in the place opposite
Damning the possibility of tides,
Screaming there are no tides in this ocean,
Pooling the past in shallow foot-prints,
Impounding the used brine . . .

Fools

And the ship fast, the hull careened,
The planks warped by the sun, the beautiful
Carved curve of the stern in the caked
Ooze and the Minoan prow
Dribbled by roosting birds . . .

Four thousand

Years of that sea-wandering brought to
This!
    Stalled!
        Stinking of sulphur!
Gas out of guts in the muck like voices
Blathering slanders in the house of
State, and the obscene birds, the black,
Indecent, dribbling, obscene birds,
Their mouths filled with excrement, shrieking,
Fouling the figure of the prow . . .

The springs of the sea, O God, where are they?

Where shall the slavered eyes be washed with
Salt, the ears with salt, the tongues
Washed with the sea-salt?

On what tide

Rising to what fresh wind, what cries
Of morning seagulls, shall the ship move;
Stir in her stench of ooze and lift
And on the cold sea, on the cleansing water,
Lean to her course?

Where are the fountains?

114

THE HERO

from Actfive

THE SHAPE OF FLESH AND BONE

The lights come up. A painted door
Opens on a painted sea
Blue as childhood's. One by one
The colored parasols appear
Delightful in remembered sun,
And under dunes beside the beach
A garden in a far-off year
Lifts silver apples out of reach.
The child beneath the tree is gone
But all the golden birds are here.
The time becomes the time before
As still as morning and as near —
Only that there sounds between
The painted waves upon the shore
The shudder of a surf not seen,
And sounds across the painted wood
A wind not lifted on the leaves,
And sounds beneath the sun the eaves
Dripping their icicles of blood.

Who is he that tiptoe in the wings
Takes breath to speak and will not show his face?

Every age must have its hero:
Even the faint age of fear —

Even here, in this belated place
Deserted by the God, wherein the King

Abandons, and the shape of Man
Lies murdered in his deeds of grace —

Every circle has its center
Where the curve is made and meant . . .

Every history returns upon its moral
As the annals of the creatures of the coral
Turn upon the turning of the surf upon the reef.

For the flesh has its belief
And the bone its expectation:
Time that turns the wheel of night
Through the iron constellation,
Time that drives the herded stars among the trees,
Turns not on the turning pole but these.

Take the form within the circle,
Take the circle in the form,
Take the stillness at the center
Where the weight of time is borne,
Where the rush of form is spent —

Take the blossom of the laurel,
Or the photograph of Saturn,
Or the pattern of the surf,
Or the circle of the reef,
Or the wheeling of the seasons round the falling of
        the leaf —
Take the sun returning always to the evenings,
And the stars in their rehearsals,
And the bell his silver verse
With its turning and returning
Like the figures on an urn —

Take the passions in a life
With the pain that turns to rapture turned to pain,
Or the cycles of the war
With the towns that burn again
And the dead that died before —

Find the point in time that turns upon itself
Like the pivot of the thrower's whirling knife
Or the wheeling of the echo of the bell!

Where the word alone is left,
Hard and secret as a shell
That the grinding sea has ground,

There what flesh and bone believe
Shapes the world that whirls them round!

There what flesh and bone — beset
From above: struck from the one side and the other:
Led by folly with its frantic fears:
Taught by hate that shrieks with stoppled ears:
Prayed for by revenge and bloody rage:
Behind, a war that smolders as it dies:
A war before them in their smoldering eyes:
The stench around them of this rotting age —

There what flesh and bone — the marble fountains
Spent, the grace gone, laughter silenced, youth
Spilt on the earth on the salt beach on the mountains,
Pain the constant lot, the daily awakening,
Beauty deprived, quiet taken,
Love a spasm on a bench, the truth
A gun butt and the church a gangster's mask:

Murder by law and falsehood in its state —
There what flesh and bone await
In the late time, in the open obscenity,
Madness private and put on, the rape of
Right from reason, charity from prayer —
There what flesh and bone attend
Shapes the world that shapes its end.

Flesh and bone —
Sojourners here in the light and the next light
And gone some morning and the embers
Cold, the grass trodden;
Strangers in the wheeling light where they alone
Of all that grows and greens do not return
With the turning of the wheel.

The blinded gunner at the ford — the rest
Dead: the rest fallen: none to see:
None to say the deed was well done: no one:
None to praise or to withhold praise: none
Ever to know or guess or speak his name —
The blinded gunner in the beaten cause
Holds the ford behind the fleeing army:
Aims at changes in the water: aims
By the wind's cold on the wound: by the pain: awk-
    wardly . . .

The responsible man, death's hand upon his shoulder,
Knowing well the liars may prevail
And calumny bring all his days to nothing;
Knowing truth has often been betrayed
By time that keeps it, as the crock taints water;
Knowing nothing suffered or endured
Will change by one word what the worst will say,

What those who listen to the worst believe —
The responsible man: teeth bad: sleep
Difficult: tired tired tired to the heart:
Carries the day to the next day to the next:
Does what must be done: dies in his chair
Fagged out, worn down, sick
With the weight of his own bones, the task finished,
The war won, the victory assured,
The glory left behind him for the others.

(And the wheels roll up through the night in the sweet
    land
In the cool air in the spring between the lanterns.)

The poor Negro delivers the laundry, refuses the
Extra nickel for carfare. I can walk —
I got my way to walk . . .

                    The sick bride,
Bedridden, gives her love to the well, comforts the
Happy, makes the town shine with her loss:
Lies all night alone with the one star
Cold in the window, waking and afraid.

The hostage hears the key turn in the lock
Not his but nearer morning after morning,
Hears the footstep stumbling on the stair,
Hears the block door shut, the bolt shot over,
Wonders which one, listens for the volley,
Walks the cell three steps and turn and three,
Smells the urine in the corner, smells
The stale potato smell of dirty stone,
Thinks Tomorrow, turns and thinks and turns:
Will not call out, will not go mad, will not

No matter how long or how many mornings,
No matter whether anyone will know,
No matter whether anyone, no matter . . .

The huge injustice: the intolerable wrong —
The life unmeant: the dying unremarked:
Multitudes mingled together in one death
And none remembered of them all: not one: —
No word or act recovered or put down
In stone or in a poem or recalled
Years afterward in peace in better times —
The eucalyptus fragrant by the water.
The huge injustice! The intolerable wrong!
Death-camp cities where beneath the night
The faceless figures wander without names
Fenced by the barbed and icy stars, and stare
Beyond them at the memory of their lives:
Vastness overwhelming all with its ignorance!

And yet the will endures: the boy dies
Believing in his death and in the others.
The woman tells her son to act the man.
The heart persists. The love survives.
The nameless flesh and bone accepts
Some duty to be beautiful and brave
Owed neither to the world nor to the grave
Nor to the stone God nor the exiled King
Nor Man, the murdered dream, nor anything
But only to the flesh the bone
The flesh that breathes the bone that stands
The eyes the hands and each alone —
Some resolution to be dutiful and good
Owed by the lost child to the dreadful wood.

The flesh that once sang
With the ardor of love
Is dumb and is mute
Where the dog stoops above
Where the dog with his jaws
In the charnel of leaves
Champs it with hate
But the flesh still believes.

The bone that once danced
In the intricate round
Of loving and giving
Is still and is bound.
The spider that stings
And the spider that weaves
Wind it with fear
But the bone still believes.

The flesh and the bone
That danced and that sang —
Fear with its web
And hate with its fang
Bind them in silence
And grind them and grieve
But the flesh and the bone
Still believe still believe.

Abandoned by the guardians and gods,
The great companion of the metaphor
Dead of the wars and wounds (O murdered dream!),
The city of man consumed to ashes, ashes,
The republic a marble rubble on its hill,
The laws rules rites prayers philters all exhausted,

Elders and the supernatural aids withdrawn —
Abandoned by them all, by all forsaken,
The naked human perishable heart —
Naked as sea-worm in the shattered shell —
No further savior standing to come forth,
Nor magic champion with miraculous blade,
Nor help in fight nor succor in the field
(Thou art my Shield! Thou art my Rock!)
No help, no hand, no succor but itself —
The human perishable heart, confused
Weak frightened in the staring face of time —
After so long a shelter shuddering cold,
After so long a slumber sleeping still —
Takes breath to speak and in the iron door
Where once the dreams stood guardian in its place
Stands guard: bears truth: knows fear and will outface,
Unarmed at last before the vast ordeal,
The death behind us and the death before.

The scene dissolves. The closet world
Collapses in enormous night.
The garden where the marble Gods
Kept music and the player Kings
Is gone and gone the golden light,
The careful lawns, the ordered trees,
Where man upon the waste of time
Enclosed his small eternities.
All this has vanished. In its stead,
Minute upon an immense plain
Where vultures huddle and the soft
And torpid rats recoil and crawl,
Gorged with a food that has no name,
And voices in the dark of air

Cry out Despair and fall and fail —
Minute upon an immense plain
The mortal flesh and mortal bone
Are left among the stones to play
The man beneath the moon alone: —
And know the part they have to bear
And know the void vast night above
And know the night below and dare
Endure and love.

THE ART

THEORY OF POETRY

Know the world by heart
Or never know it!
Let the pedant stand apart —
Nothing he can name will show it:
Also him of intellectual art.
None know it
Till they know the world by heart.

Take heart then, poet!

VICISSITUDES
OF THE CREATOR

Fish has laid her succulent eggs
Safe in Saragossa weed
So wound and bound that crabbed legs
Nor clattering claws can find and feed.

Thus fish commits unto the sea
Her infinite future and the Trade
Blows westward toward eternity
The universe her love has made.

But when, upon this leeward beach,
The measureless sea journey ends
And ball breaks open, from the breach
A deft, gold, glossy crab extends

In ring-side ritual of self-applause
The small ironic silence of his claws.

A MAN'S WORK

An apple-tree, a cedar and an oak
Grow by the stone house in the rocky field
Where I write poems when my hand's in luck.
The cedar I put in: the rest are wild —

Wind dropped them. Apples strew the autumn ground
With black, sweet-smelling pips. The oak strews air,
Summers with shadow, winters with harsh sound.
The cedar's silent with its fruit to bear.

WITH AGE WISDOM

At twenty, stooping round about,
I thought the world a miserable place,
Truth a trick, faith in doubt,
Little beauty, less grace.

Now at sixty what I see,
Although the world is worse by far,
Stops my heart in ecstasy.
God, the wonders that there are!

WAKING

The sadness we bring back from sleep
like an herb in the mouth . . .

                    sage?

                            rosemary?

like a fragrance we can neither lose nor
keep . . .

          woodsmoke?

                oak-leaves?

like the closing
softly of a distant . . .

               distant? . . .

                    door . . .

                          Oh

like earth on our shoes from an unremembered
    journey . . .
What earth?

            What journey?

                Why did we return?

SEEING

BY NIGHT

What did you see, Cromarty, by the house
or where the house once was?

                         A tree.

I know it hurts. I have to ask you.

I said I saw a tree.

                    What kind of
tree?

         A pear tree.

                  Look here, soldier!
Look! We drop a flare. You see . . .
what do you see?

                 A pear. A tree . . .

I told you I was sorry . . .

                      . . . tree
bloom in the night.

                  And that was all?

No. I saw a petal fall.

Think! You haven't long, Cromarty.

I thought! Good God, I thought! I thought,
Christ! I'd never seen a tree!

And that was all . . . ?

(2)
AT THE SATURDAY CLUB

Harlow: Our generation discovered the universe.

Robert: That's why we're lost.

Harlow: Men before us
        Thought in beginnings and ends, all of them.
        Nobody knew that time is a circle,
        that space is a circle, that space-time
        closes the circle.

Robert: They weren't lost.

Harlow: They didn't know they were lost but they were:
        they were wrong.

Robert: And we're right and we're lost.

Harlow: When you're right
            you can't be lost: you know where you are.

Robert: You know where you are when you're lost.

Harlow: Where?

Robert: Lost.

132

(3)
IN THE EAST

Why are you moving your lips, said the Emperor I Tsung.
I am blessing the prophets, said Ibn Wahab the traveler.

Where are the prophets, said the Emperor I Tsung.
    I do not see them.

You see them, said Ibn Wahab the traveler:
    you do not recognize them but you see them.

I see a man in a boat on a great ocean, said the Emperor
    I Tsung.

That, said Ibn Wahab the traveler, is Noah
    who swam on the world when the Flood drowned it.

I see a man in the fields, said the Emperor I Tsung:
    he is wandering.

That is Abraham, said Ibn Wahab the traveler:
    he is wandering everywhere looking for God.

I see a man on a tree, said the Emperor I Tsung.

That, said Ibn Wahab the traveler, is Jesus.

What did he do, said the Emperor I Tsung:
    did he swim on the world? Did he wander everywhere?

He died, said Ibn Wahab the traveler.

Why do I weep, said the Emperor I Tsung.

You have recognized Jesus, said Ibn Wahab the traveler.

(4)
At the Dark's Edge

Sister tree,
deaf and dumb and blind, and we
have ears to hear, have eyes for sight,
and yet our sister tree can find,
fumbling deaf and groping blind,
with field before her and with wood behind,
what we can't . . .
light.

THE METAPHOR

from Hypocrite Auteur, mon semblable, mon frère

A world ends when its metaphor has died.

An age becomes an age, all else beside,
When sensuous poets in their pride invent
Emblems for the soul's consent
That speak the meanings men will never know
But man-imagined images can show:
It perishes when those images, though seen,
No longer mean.

A world was ended when the womb
Where girl held God became the tomb
Where God lies buried in a man:
Botticelli's image neither speaks nor can
To our kind. His star-guided stranger
Teaches no longer, by the child, the manger,
The meaning of the beckoning skies.

Sophocles, when his reverent actors rise
To play the king with bleeding eyes,
No longer shows us on the stage advance
God's purpose in the terrible fatality of chance.

No woman living, when the girl and swan
Embrace in verses, feels upon
Her breast the awful thunder of that breast
Where God, made beast, is by the blood confessed.

Empty as conch shell by the waters cast
The metaphor still sounds but cannot tell,
And we, like parasite crabs, put on the shell
And drag it at the sea's edge up and down.

This is the destiny we say we own.

The journey of our history has not ceased:
Earth turns us still toward the rising east,
The metaphor still struggles in the stone,
The allegory of the flesh and bone
Still stares into the summer grass
That is its glass,
The ignorant blood
Still knocks at silence to be understood.

Poets, deserted by the world before,
Turn round into the actual air:
Invent the age! Invent the metaphor!

REASONS FOR MUSIC

for Wallace Stevens

Why do we labor at the poem
Age after Age — even an age like
This one, when the living rock
No longer lives and the cut stone perishes? —

Hölderlin's question. Why be poet
Now when the meanings do not mean? —
When the stone shape is shaped stone? —
Dürftiger Zeit? — time without inwardness?

Why lie upon our beds at night
Holding a mouthful of words, exhausted
Most by the absence of the adversary?

Why be poet? Why be man!

Far out in the uttermost Andes
Mortised enormous stones are piled.
What is man? Who founds a poem
In the rubble of wild world — wilderness.

The acropolis of eternity that crumbles
Time and again is mine — my task.
The heart's necessity compels me:
Man I am: poet must be.

The labor of order has no rest:
To impose on the confused, fortuitous
Flowing away of the world, Form —
Still, cool, clean, obdurate,

Lasting forever, or at least
Lasting: a precarious monument
Promising immortality, for the wing
Moves and in the moving balances.

Why do we labor at the poem?
Out of the turbulence of the sea,
Flower by brittle flower, rises
The coral reef that calms the water.

Generations of the dying
Fix the sea's dissolving salts
In stone, still trees, their branches immovable,
Meaning
        the movement of the sea.

THE INFINITE REASON

(1)

Rilke thought it was the human part
To translate planet into angel —
Bacteria of mortal heart

Fermenting into something rich and strange,
The orchard at home, the sky above Toledo:
Sight into soul was what we lived to change.

The key, he told us, was the angel's need,
Not our necessity — and yet
No angel answered for *his* heart to feed.

(2)

The truth is nearer to the true than that.
The truth is, the necessity is ours.
Man is creature to whom meaning matters.

Until we read these faces, figures, flowers,
These shapes averted from us that all vanish,
Everything vanishes — a swarm of hours

Swirling about a bonfire that began
When? Why? To end where? And for what?

(3)

Miser of meanings in the stars, O man
Who finds the poem moonlight has forgotten!

Eternity is what our wanderers gather,
Image by image, out of time — the cut

Branch that flowers in the bowl. Our father,
Thou who ever shalt be, the poor body
Dying at every ditch hath borne Thee, Father.

(4)

Our human part is to redeem the god
Drowned in this time of space, this space
That time encloses.

                    From the Tyrrhenian flood

The floated marble, the cold human face!

ARS POETICA

A poem should be palpable and mute
As a globed fruit,

Dumb
As old medallions to the thumb,

Silent as the sleeve-worn stone
Of casement ledges where the moss has grown —

A poem should be worldless
As the flight of birds.

*

A poem should be motionless in time
As the moon climbs,

Leaving, as the moon releases
Twig by twig the night-entangled trees,

Leaving, as the moon behind the winter leaves,
Memory by memory the mind —

A poem should be motionless in time
As the moon climbs.

*

A poem should be equal to:
Not true.

For all the history of grief
An empty doorway and a maple leaf.

For love
The leaning grasses and two lights above the sea —

A poem should not mean
But be.

WORDS IN TIME

Bewildered with the broken tongue
Of wakened angels in our sleep —
Then, lost the music that was sung
And lost the light time cannot keep!

There is a moment when we lie
Bewildered, wakened out of sleep,
When light and sound and all reply:
That moment time must tame and keep.

That moment, like a flight of birds
Flung from the branches where they sleep,
The poet with a beat of words
Flings into time for time to keep.

NEWS FROM ELSEWHERE

IF GOD IS GOD
from *J.B.*

I heard upon his dry dung heap
That man cry out who cannot sleep:
"If God is God He is not good,
If God is good He is not God;
Take the even, take the odd,
I would not sleep here if I could
Except for the little green leaves in the wood
And the wind on the water."

145

WHAT EVE SANG*

Space-time

Is all there is of space and time
But is not all. There is a rhyme
For all of space and all of time.

I heard it on that Eden night
The branching tree stood dark alight
Like willow in the wind, so white
Its unknown apples on the night:

I heard beyond that tree a tree
Stir in silence over me.
In space and time, eyes only see,
Ears only hear, the green-wood tree:

But Oh! I heard the whole of time
And all of space give ringing rhyme
And ring and ring and chime and chime
When I reached out to touch and climb
In spite of space, in spite of time.

* This poem and the following seventeen poems are from *Songs for Eve*.

WHAT EVE SAID

Eve said:
From tree to tree
Will journey be;
The one, she said,
Alive and green,
The other dead,
And what's between,
Eve said,
Our lives mean.

Eve said:
With tree began
That traveller, man;
With tree, she said,
Will journey end.
That tree, though dead,
Its leaves will spend,
Eve said,
World without end.

Eve said:
The first is his
Whose world this is:
The last, she said,
Blossomed and blown
Though wood be dead,
Is mine, my own.
Eve said:
O my son! O my son!

EVE'S EXILE

Eden was an endless place,
Time enough for all of space
And space for all that time to pass.

We lived in time as fishes live
Within the lapsing of the wave
That with the water's moving move.

We lived in space as hawk in air:
The place we were was everywhere
And everywhere we were, we were.

Fish and hawk have eyes of glass
Wherein the skies and waters pass
As in a glass the images —

They mirror but they may not see.
When I had tasted fruit of tree
Fish and hawk, they fled from me:

"She has a watcher in her eyes,"
The hawk screamed from the steep of skies,
Fish from sea-deep where he lies.

Our exile is our eyes that see.
Hawk and fish have eyes but we
Behold what they can only be.

Space within its time revolves
But Eve must spin as Adam delves
Because our exile is ourselves.

EVE ANSWERS THE BURDOCK

What did I eat when I ate apple?
What did I eat in the sweet
Day, in the leaves' dapple?
Eve.

What did I know when I knew apple?
What did I know in the new
Night, in the stars' stipple?
Eve.

WHAT THE VINE SAID
TO EVE

Man is the leaky bung
That lets the ferment in:
The wine were sweet and young
But for your sin.

But for your fault the wine
Were sweet as water is:
No taint of taste, no sign,
No promises.

But for your sin no tongue
Had tasted, salt as blood,
The certainty among
These grapes of God.

THE FALL!

                    said Eve;
That Fall began
What leaves conceive
Nor fishes can —
So far a flight
Past touch, past sight.

Get down, said Eve
Upon your shins,
Upon your shanks,
And pray reprieve,
And give God thanks
For Eden sins.

The Fall! she said —
From earth to God!
Give thanks, said she, for branch, for bole,
For Eve who found the grace to fall
From Adam, browsing animal,
Into the soaring of the soul!

EVE'S NOW-I-LAY-ME

To separate myself from space
I gave the water pool my face:
To separate myself from time
I gave the stars my soul to climb.

150

ADAM IN THE EVENING

Beauty cannot be shown
But only at remove:
What's beautiful is known
By opposites, as love.

Counter, the mind can see.
When first Eve disobeyed
And turned and looked at me,
Beauty was made.

That distance in the blood
Whereby the eyes have sight
Is love — not understood
But infinite.

EVE IN THE DAWN

Time created out of clay
That animal with whom I lay.

Like she of wolf or lion's she
In season he would tumble me,

Yet touched me never till he took
The apple from my hand and Look!

Look! he said, your eyes that see
My eyes have images of me!

That night until the next of day
We touched in love and loving lay:

We were awake then who had slept.
Our bodies out of Eden leapt

Together to a lifted place
Past space of time and time of space

That neither space nor time had made.
There first we laughed, were first afraid.

Was it Adam, only he,
Bred that flowering branch of me
Whereon shall hang eternity?

EVE'S CHILD

Does anyone know, says Eve, that fable
Women in their dotage tell
Of girls covered by gods, unable
After to call the babe?
What pipped and tapped in Leda's shell
Laid by the shoal there in the fable?

The soul that comes from God, one says,
And one remembers him as swan
Because the swan has feathery ways,
And one as bull, so brisk the blaze,
But none remembers him as man.
It was a man took me, Eve says.

Women, when a child is found,
Make the sea sound: Hush! Hush!
Does anyone know why they make that sound?
Our blood is salt as the sea around,
Our body, at each beginning, fish:
Hush! says Eve, when a child is found.

ADAM'S JEALOUSY:
EVE'S ANSWER

Cover that infant's mouth and eyes,
Said Adam, softly where it lies:
The soul that lurks, the soul that flies,
Will enter where it clucks and cries.

Hold close, said Adam, in the leaves,
That struggling girl who first conceives.
The souls are fluttering at the eaves:
They enter flesh when flesh believes.

The invisible souls, now Eden's lost,
Hunt, he said, the chosen host
To house them, body sick with ghost.
I fear the souls, said Adam, most.

Adam, Adam, there are none
Enter flesh but flesh and bone.

Flesh and bone have wonder done
And wonder, bone and flesh are One.

EVE'S REBUKE TO HER CHILD

Who said you were bred
Not of flesh and of bone
But of somebody flown
From a place in the sky
Had no thew and no thigh
And no pelt and no poll?
Who told you that lie
About body and soul?

You think it was I,
Not that girl in the tower,
Was had by a shower
Of gold from the sky?
We do what we can!
There was none lay with me
But was made like a man
As a man ought to be.

You came by the soul
As you came by the skin
Where the raging strikes in
And the wrestlers must roll.
If you'd rather be more
You can brag if you'd rather:
Make your mother a whore,
Have a ghost for a father.

But O, the noon day
And O, the green tree!
Body of me

In the fern where we lay!
The flight that was flown
From the place in the sky —
The flesh and the bone
Made those wings that could fly.

EVE QUIETS HER CHILDREN

Eve, our mother, care and keep!
We who call you cannot sleep.

Wake then! Weep!

Eve, our mother, all the rest
Sleep about us, bird and beast.

Waking's best.

All things other turn and twine
Like gnats in atmospheres of wine.

Eden's sign!

Stars that circle in their sleep
Silver solemn statutes keep.

Stars! Time's sheep!

Suns and moons and nails and claws
Sleep out time's revolving laws.

Time! Time was!

Eve, our mother, what was wrought
Broke the sleep when we were got?

Sleep's green tree was cut, was cut.

Eve, Eve, who are we,
Born to wake and waking see?

Wake and see!

THE SERPENT'S CRADLE SONG

You are the children of Eve by the apple.
By the pip of the apple she came to conceive.
Adam, that cuckold, never begot you.
You are the children of Eve
By the apple.

Adam was hot
In the heat of the day,
And he lay in her lap
And she gave him his way,
But the pip of the apple
I taught her to eat
(Tart? — sweet!)
Was quick in her womb.
When Adam came knocking
The inn had no room.

156

Said the king to the cock:
When the day comes to bloom
Be quiet for once!
I must sleep in the tomb.
Said the king to the huntsman:
Quiet your horn!
Let the day begin dumb:
There is sleep to be born.
But the pip of the apple
Was quick in his blood:
Eve's children can sleep
But not well — not for good.

EVE OLD

The taste of time is sweet at first,
Then salt as tears, then tame as water:
Time to the old tastes bitter, bitter.

No child of mine may quench his thirst
However deep he drink of time,
Sweet or bitter, salt or tame.

Because my tongue that apple durst
His tongue shall want what time is not —
Not tame, not bitter, salt nor sweet:

Because my tongue that apple durst
Eternity shall be his thirst.

EVE'S FIRST PROPHECY

God who made the garden green
Made the apple tree to lean
And glitter in that shine and sheen.

The apple tree will fall away.

Straight of bole and strict of bough,
Sons of mine will shape and hew
Tree that Eden never knew.

The dry tree branch will swing and sway.

All to this my sons are born:
To hew and shape and raise that tree,
And stand beneath in scorn, in scorn . . .
And on it bear eternity.

The apple tree shall fall away.

The dry tree branch shall swing and sway.

EVE'S SECOND PROPHECY

This sun at last will stand and stare
And blaze and burn its planets out,
And all God's works of skill and care
Will strew the starry sky about,
Yet hearts remain what once they were.

When nothing lives of all this light
But, somewhere between star and star,
A greater darkness on the night
Where once our glimmering signals were,
What heart has seen will still be sight.

Eden's tree will wither up,
And char and in its ashes drift,
But not one leaf will wilt or drop
From that dry tree my children lift
To bear the heart's rebellious hope.

WHAT THE WIND SAID TO THE WATER:
WHAT THE WATER REPLIED

Man, like any creature,
Dies where two days meet:
Dead, by time is eaten.

Sea worm leaves behind
Shell for wave to find:
Man, the shell of mind.

Like any creature, man
Lives by luck and vanishes:
The chance wind takes the candle.

No creature leaves behind
Husk or shell or rind
Obdurate as the mind.

Life is luck, death random.

Tell me, what is man
That immortal order can?

CREATOR

The world was made by someone else,
not God. The moist, inexplicable bees,
the crystal stones, the painted shells,
the lights beyond the swarming Pleiades —

God knows nothing of these things.
We found him in the burning bush
above the desert where he sings
as flames do, trilling in their fiery hush.

He told us where the end was, knew
the way to reach it, showed the path:
there men like marigolds, he said, come true
and understand their lives and live their death.

We help each other through the blind
tall night beneath the infinite spaces:
God looks before and we behind
but somewhere else that other unknown face is.